Toward the Authentic Church

Orthodox Christians Discuss Their Conversion:
A Collection of Essays

Edited by Thomas Doulis

LIGHT & LIFE PUBLISHING
Minneapolis, Minnesota
1996

Light and Life Publishing
P.O. Box 26421
Minneapolis, Minnesota 55426-0421

ISBN 1-880971-10-0

The world has changed mightily since *Journeys to Orthodoxy*, the last collection of essays, was published. In international politics, the poisonous world of the Cold War has "thawed" in a climatic change unlike the previous, and short-lived, "Thaws" that tormented us in the past. The terrain before us now is like that left when a glacier retreats, full of ugly chasms and imposing vistas, but a land, finally, where instant annihilation is not a daily possibility.

The world of Orthodox Christianity has also been changed. The third great wave of persecution has now abated. Pagan Rome is no more; Islam, that had surrounded, dominated, and enslaved millions of Orthodox Christians, is now battling with a world that it believes has cornered it; and Soviet Communism, which had had a stranglehold on Russia and the lands of Eastern and Central Europe, has now become an ever-receding nightmare.

For more than seven decades Russia was dominated by a system that tried to destroy every vestige of the Church; yet, within a few years of the regime's collapse, the number of baptisms, marriages, and other sacraments has increased ten-fold, churches are being restored, and monasteries are being rebuilt and repopulated. There have been martyrs, certainly, and the gulags were filled with dissenters, rebels, and the merely unlucky, but it was the *babushkas*, taking their grandchildren to be secretly baptized during the seven decades of terror, who kept the apparently withered and moribund Church living and ever-green, ready to flourish and bring fourth fruit when the climate changed.

Our own legal and political climate has been more hospitable to the practice of religion. Yet there is something about life in a secular and rationalistic world that makes the religious orientation suspect. To express an interest in religious issues is to run the risk of being quickly categorized as an "extremist" or a "fundamentalist." "Try talking about God at an English dinner party," Margaret Long suggests, "and watch the faces glaze in silent disbelief." Apparently it is only in the "context of satirical allusion" that discussion about beliefs can be considered as anything less than a "social gaffe." The attitude toward believers in university circles, Barbara Newman offers, ranges from "mild contempt to benign amusement" and has forced her to live in "a kind of spiritual schizophrenia."

Perhaps it is easier to resist an aggressively secular world when the leaders who embody its principles are tyrannical and brutal. The world they represent is so abhorrent that the mysteries of religion, especially one that expresses the love of a philanthropic God, beckon as assurances that the lives of men and women are inherently beautiful, valuable, and important. In his famous 1842 essay, "The Transcendentalist," Emerson says something about the numbed view we have toward the world's mystery when we allow secular and free market principles to stifle our sense of awe.

> *The sturdy capitalist, no matter how deep and square on blocks of Quincy marble he lays the foundations of his banking-house or Exchange, must set it, at last, not on a cube corresponding to the angles of his structure, but on a mass of unknown materials and solidity, red-hot or white-hot perhaps at the core, which rounds off to an almost perfect sphericity, and lies floating in soft air, and goes spinning away, dragging bank and banker with it at a rate of thousands of miles the hour, he knows not whither – a bit of bullet, now glimmering, now darkling through a small cubic space on the edge of an unimaginable pit of emptiness.*

In our youth most of us sense this creative disorientation. We are struck by the disparity between ordinary life – buildings set "deep and square on blocks of Quincy marble" – and the awesomeness of living on this "mass of unknown materials" we call the earth that spins away "at a rate of thousands of miles an hour." As we "mature," though, we either ignore this disparity or are satisfied by the current scientific explanations. Few of us change our ways or our thoughts.

Those who go through a conversion experience, though, are very conscious of the way they change and the reasons for it. The conversion experience is often, and inaccurately, considered a violent one, Saint Paul's blindness on the road to Damascus being its model and William James's *The Varieties of Religious Experience* its text. The gradual conversion, though, which the essays in this collection represent, is a much more interesting phenomenon. As Father A. James Bernstein says, his "encounter with God didn't involve visions, voices, or spectacular incidents," but came to him, instead, as "a light... in the darkness of my heart." All of the present writers slowly matured into a belief in the values, customs, dogmas, and traditions of the Orthodox Church.

Nancy Forest-Flier, more than any other contributor, provides a positive response to Reformed Christianity by granting that within it she was made "aware of the Important Questions in life" and felt "a deep hunger to answer those questions." Her narrative is rich in imagery and perception, while the "polar vision" that struck her as she stepped down from the school bus at her corner in New Jersey reminds us of Emerson's insight into life's mystery. She feels "the world as a globe, and I could feel it turning around," a sensation she re-encounters in the poetry of Wallace Stevens and, in Jerusalem, in the Church of the Transfiguration. The vision teaches her that "the kingdom of God is here, right now, within you." She needs "to be in a fertile place where the deepest questions about the most basic human condition were at home" and wants a religion that would advance "into every corner of your life and lay claim to it." A student of literature, she traces the etymology of "free" and constructs a simple and elegant route to God, since "free" means "dear to the chief," i.e., "loved by God." Like most of the other contributors, she finds herself dissatisfied by a Christianity that emphasizes social awareness rather than prayer, which is ironic since both she and her husband have, more than most Christians, been involved in social programs like the Fellowship of Reconciliation.

Fr. A. James Bernstein in "Orthodoxy: Jewish and Christian" emphasizes his need for the *continuity* with Old Testament worship and practice that he found in the Orthodox Church; this commitment has not alienated him from his Jewish roots, which are justly powerful, for on his way he was involved with that interesting group, "Jews for Jesus," now based in San Francisco. In his essay, the reader sees the careful enumeration of Old Testament practices that translate directly into the embedded order of the Early Church, which built on the legacy of Jewish Christians. The ornate beauty of Orthodox churches, according to him, is in the direct tradition of the Temple, and he cites the relevant textual passages to prove his assertions. These citations must be seen as arguments *against* the iconoclastic instincts embedded within Reformed Christianity as well as *for* the Jewish legacy within Orthodox Christian worship. In his journey to Orthodox Christianity, Father James has had to pass though Evangelical Protestantism, which emphasizes faith and works but not worship or its mystery. Since his encounter with Roman Christianity occurred after Vatican II, he did not study Roman Catholicism and, when he exhibited an interest, found the folk-masses too casual. He needed the structure of ritual, of the "Temple worship," which his years in Evangelical Protestantism had almost convinced him was "something corrupt" and its "beauty... somehow suspect."

Bill Barlow's contribution narrates the growth of a man from an evangelical background through various stages: soldier, soldier of God, postulant attracted to the monastic vocation, and finally Orthodox soldier. He, too, rejected the efforts to make religion "relevant" and palatable by denuding it of ritual and beauty. In his time, these efforts were expressed in slogans like "mankind had come of age" and demanded a "religionless Christianity," which entailed "secularizing the Gospel." But he had other loyalties and commitments, and they seem to be the fruition of a childhood spent admiring the imagery of military service – uniforms, regimental badges, drill – which were emblems of fidelity and devotion to a cause we now, a half century after the Second World War, continue to see as a moral struggle of titanic dimensions. In the Irish Guards, he found "no contradiction in being both a soldier and a Christian," and he asserts that being a disciplined soldier, "turning the other cheek" to "those in authority," allowed him to practice "non-resistance" *without* becoming a pacifist. In what might strike us as paradoxical, the statement that "the Gospel... is bigger than pacifism" sets us firmly in the tradition of those equestrian and warrior saints who defended the Church against its enemies and in most cases perished as martyrs for their steadfastness. His intellectual world, with reference to *Good-bye to All That* by Robert Graves, the fiction of John Masters, and memoirs of various wars, presents to us a different but nevertheless compelling view of Christianity.

Jim Forest, a "red-diaper baby," son of nominal atheists who in other circumstances would have been believers, would certainly disagree with

Bill Barlow about the tension between pacifism and Christianity. He worked his way through the political traumas of the Cold War era, often paying profoundly for parents who were communists, a father who was unjustly imprisoned for six months, a mother who tried to bring up her sons with the ever-present threat of job loss poisoning her days. Nature, too, provided him with the sense of awe that, he believes, "is a religious state of mind," but it was the emotional experience he had during and after watching a film of a nun's failed vocation that he felt "an uncomplicated and overwhelming happiness" and sensed that, "for the first time" in his life that "the blackness beyond the stars" – Emerson's "unimaginable pit of emptiness" – was not "terrifying."

Drawn to ritual and tradition, he experimented with Roman Catholicism and Episcopalianism. He visited a Greek Orthodox cathedral, but in the late 1950s, the ethnic element was still overpowering and off-putting, as was race in the black church, to which he was also drawn. He chose the Roman Catholic faith, but this was the time of Vatican II and all the august agelessness of the Latin rite was to be jettisoned for a liturgy devised, he says, "by committee" and music that was "fit for shopping malls and Disneyland."

It is clear that he could not remain in the navy. He sought a discharge as a conscientious objector, joined the Catholic Worker movement, and was deeply influenced by those beacons, Dorothy Day and Thomas Merton, both Catholic converts and both powerfully drawn to Orthodox mysticism and iconography. His interest in social and political activism is strong and his presence in world Orthodoxy is inspiring to those who want to see religion take a creative role in the daily events of the post Cold-War world.

Sister Nonna (Verna Harrison before being tonsured a *rassophore* nun) wondered if another cause besides heredity and environment could be responsible for the "mystery of human personhood" and was drawn, in physics and astronomy, to questions about "the origins of the universe," and, in mathematics, to "different kinds of infinity." These questions of "why" rather than "how" are essentially theological and, after acknowledging the *possibility* of God's existence and, praying that He "do with me as (He) will," felt her "whole perception of reality change" and "caught a glimpse of the world transfigured." She provides us with a countdown of her awareness of God's immanence. On her journey to Orthodoxy, though, she proved her deeply held theological principles in her resistance to the belief in the Bible's inerrancy held by her evangelical colleagues and studied the Church Fathers to find confirmation in her ideas. Her struggle to reconcile this sense of presence and transfiguration with her personal needs emerge in her need to worship as a monastic.

Barbara Newman surprises us. We are more accustomed to reading about women who identify themselves as "feminist intellectuals" espousing secular virtues than a God-centered way of thought. But the careful reader will not be tricked by her cool and droll manner into thinking that she is any less serious than the others in her quest for authenticity and meaning. In her essay, we see the battle of a literary woman against a world that refuses to conform to her expectation of a "dramatic conversion like those William James had written about." No visions appeared to her, alas, and the world of the Seventies she lived in – Oberlin College, Transcendental Meditation, liturgical dance, University of Chicago, Yale – could not accommodate the religious experiences that culture had taught her to expect as authentic. Her "festivity" priest counseled her against baptism in her condition of *angst*, and she writes that "certainty was what I demanded and that, above all, God wished to deny." She is a medievalist, and as time passes will, I am sure, become an important one, and though she emerges from the secular and Enlightenment Jewish tradition, whose intellectual contributions have enhanced the world of letters and science, she has found in the Orthodox Christian way of life a meaning that has enriched her. Moreover, she is unique in this collection in bringing up a way of looking at theology and worship from a feminist perspective that must be considered by all well-meaning Orthodox Christians.

The first time reader of Margaret Viscountess Long's work will no doubt be struck by her extraordinary sensitivity to color, fragrance, and shape – most often of a botanical, but occasionally of an entomological, nature. She sees the world through the eyes of an artist, and the major stages in her life seem to be illuminated by attraction to, and repulsion from, objects and courses of action that represent another sort of understanding. In fact, her first book, *Let the Petals Fall*, was she feared heretical, and she admits, with becoming disquiet, the product of a stage in her life when she was learning from revelation and searched for "purpose" in "obscure natural phenomena." But many of the contributors to this collection were enabled by insights from the natural world to sense hints of Nature's God behind Nature herself. And her world, Establishment Britain was inhospitable to serious discussion of religion. "You knew (God) was important but nobody had introduced you," and you, diffident and proper, were compelled to pretend that He did not exist lest you blunder socially. She learned early that "mystery" and "stillness" are "the natural environment through which God could act" but in the arcane and socially hierarchical world of British aristocracy these attributes were difficult to come by. Religion in the 1960s was "an accepted, rather formal obligation" but "inspiration depended on the eloquence of the sermon or the loudness of the hymn singing."

Fr. Daniel Matheson found himself undergoing greater discomfort in the ministry as the United Church of Canada began to abandon central doctrines of Christianity. He was born on the Feast of Theophany, the "old Christmas" as his mother called it, and baptized in the parish church of Saint Columba, a name that harks back to Celtic Christianity, whose beliefs in the One, Holy, and Apostolic Church were, by definition, Orthodox. He was given an old style ministerial training: Classical Greek, philosophy, systematic theology, homiletics, Old and New Testament. Then, during the Second World War and with his new wife, he was sent to the frozen and trackless north to minister to a native settlement "more primitive than what we now identify as 'Third World'." What he writes about is his painful course, one motivated by a deep need to worship in the "right way," that eventually led him to Orthodoxy, a road he followed even though he had few obvious landmarks on his way. His family was surprised and dismayed by his and his wife's decision to convert, but when the "turn" had been completed, his daughter acknowledged to him that "you have always been Orthodox." His words on language, which to some converts is a daunting obstacle, are instructive and self-effacing. "We whose native tongue is English can be so stubborn about language!"

Bishop Kallistos of Diokleia, known to many readers as Timothy Ware before his entry into the monastic life and elevation to the episcopacy, recalls precisely his first encounter with Orthodoxy. He had walked out of the brilliant sunshine into a darkened Gothic church, now demolished, and witnessed the Slavonic liturgy of a Russian Orthodox congregation. It was beauty and mystery that won him over, but it was the "living and unbroken continuity with the Church of the Apostles and Martyrs" that held him.

Like most people hovering around the edges of commitment, he received mixed messages at the time from clerics and hierarchs who were fearful that converts might not be integrated into the living community of their ethnic parishes and were reluctant to throw them into "the deep end of the Orthodox swimming-pool," leaving them "to their own devices to sink or swim." It was suggested that he "remain a member of the Anglican Church" until reconciliation between the churches was effected, since it was better that Anglicans, rather than convert individually, act as an "Anglo-Orthodox leaven" within their present churches.

He pursued his studies of Classical and New Testament Greek, meeting Orthodox thinkers and reading their works, finding himself inexorably drawn to the Orthodox Church because of the fullness of her witness to Christ as expressed and embodied in Holy Tradition. As a layman he wanted the *fullness, wholeness*, and *Tradition*, the "unbroken continuity" that the Orthodox Church represented; as an Orthodox bishop, it is within the scope of his authority to assure and maintain these.

The laity in the United States, embedded as we are in the fragmented multiplicity of jurisdictions, will be surprised to learn that the same issues that plague Orthodoxy in the Western Hemisphere are still evident – and more so in the 1950s – in the British Isles and on the Continent. In his forty years as an Orthodox Christian, however, Bishop Kallistos has seen the hope of a *rapprochement* between the Anglican and Orthodox churches fade as innovations within the former have totally changed the terrain and terms of discourse.

But he wonders if the jurisdictional pluralism may not be "at best a provisional arrangement... no more than temporary and transitional"; at any rate, this pluralism served him well when he was ready to convert, since it enabled him to evade the dilemma of choosing between the Russian Orthodox Church in Exile, to which – because of its martyrdom under the Soviets – he was drawn and the Russian Orthodox Church Outside of Russia, under the jurisdiction of the Moscow Patriarchate and susceptible to Soviet pressures. He joined the Greek diocese in Britain under the Patriarch of Constantinople and, in what may prove to be a far-sighted historical insight, reasons that "when eventually the Orthodox in western Europe achieve organizational unity" a prospect not at all so inconceivable in the near future, judging by the vigorous leadership exerted by Bartholomeos I, it "could only happen under the pastoral protection of the Ecumenical Throne."

It should be expected that a strong-minded and interesting group of people would express ideas that we might find challenging, but I've limited my role as editor to asking the writers to make their less accessible statements clearer so that the lay reader would be able to understand them more readily. Stylistic changes have been kept to a minimum. Though I've encountered editorial difficulties in the essays of our British contributors who were unfamiliar with, or resisted, American spellings, I have tried to respect idiomatic differences.

To generalize somewhat I'd say that several writers were put off by the ethnic element in Orthodoxy. None of these, interestingly enough, was an American, or, in deference to Father Daniel, a citizen of the United States. In fact, Bishop Kallistos, who had no choice but to select an ethnic diocese, accepted the Greek, though drawn to the Russians, *because* he'd been a student of Classical and New Testament Greek and would have been uncomfortable with Church Slavonic. Try as we might to respect the ideal of "the melting pot," Americans seem reluctant to accept the "foreign" in religion. One rejects "Greek ethnocentrism," while another does not wish to "convert to Greek or Russian culture" in order to live as an Orthodox Christian. The issue is not iconography, as it might have been half a century ago when the culture had not quite absorbed and digested the austere rigidity and restricted palette of Byzantium and Holy Russia. Now, even those painters not formally Orthodox are attracted to the Orthodox style of pictorial representation. The issue is language, a more intractable problem.

"For some people," one writer observes, "worship in an ancient language is a barrier." But there is ambivalence, too, since on his way to Orthodox worship the same writer grew to "love the Latin" of pre-Vatican II days, learned Latin prayers by heart, and invested so much emotion in the language –perhaps because it is dead? – that when the mass had been "Englished" the Roman church, he claims, lost "not only Latin but Gregorian chant" as well.

What to do about an issue so important to our co-religionists? It would be easy to counter that the same things happened in American Orthodoxy. When some Orthodox jurisdictions "Englished" the liturgy, they lost not only the language but the exquisite beauty and spiritual grandeur of the music in which the chants were embedded. And this goes beyond the question of what to do with the "left over syllables" when English words do not match the traditional melody of the chant. Instead of music "fit for shopping malls and Disneyland," to use Jim Forest's phrase, we are often presented with monotonous repetitions that reject the hymnology that the Church has passed on to us as a legacy of the two millennia of her past. As Theodore Bogdanos, an eminent church composer, has written, the problem is initially syntactical. "English, with its many consonants (twice as many as in Latin or Greek) and its inflexible sentence structure (subject-verb-object), could not fit the flowing, ornate Gregorian melodies," or the soaring Byzantine music, "which thrived on the many open vowels and the immensely flexible word order" of the ancient languages.

Yet little can delight or startle us more than the splendid and towering expression of our longing for God and God's reaching out to us, which is the liturgy and the readings ancillary to it, presented in *our* language, after years of having been encrypted in a tongue we may think we understand but may not be able to fully respond to with emotion and spiritual clarity.

We may not see the solution to this problem in our lifetime. We may need to wander, parched and feverish in an aesthetic desert for forty years before we hear the liquid sounds of the oasis we left as the older generation of chanters died. The demands of Orthodox worship are rich and varied, however, and Orthodox composers, of which there are quite a few, seem to be emerging to lead us out of our quandary. Everything, I am sure, will be worked out eventually. Those who have jettisoned the culture (though a careful and honest appraisal will show that there are many vestiges of its past a jurisdiction retains after its hierarchs think they have "ethnically purged" it) will develop one of their own, and those who have retained the culture of their country of origin will, even in the ethnically dense Eastern United States, need eventually to adapt to America.

What is needed, clearly, is an *American* Orthodoxy and an end to what some have termed "the scandal" of jurisdictions. When this will happen anyone would be foolish to predict, but it will come about. Until then, as Father Daniel says, "Orthodoxy is Orthodoxy, whatever the language of the liturgy."

Table of Contents

Right Where I'm Standing

by Nancy Forest-Flier

I grew up in New Jersey in a family that was deeply rooted in the Reformed Church, a small main-stream Protestant denomination with roots in the Dutch Reformed Church. In the 1950s, most of the members of our church were still children and grandchildren of Dutch immigrants. We went to church twice on Sunday, we all attended Sunday School and my parents were teachers, we rushed off to church again on Wednesday night after supper for "Family Night" which included catechism and choir practice, I was president of my Youth Fellowship and my parents were both youth group leaders. Our church was our spiritual and social center.

But for me, church was more than habit or social matrix or ethnic identity. It was a rich, Biblical, prayer-filled atmosphere which encouraged the asking of important questions. Like other churches, our church communicated its theology by means of certain phrases which contained essential truths and were easily taught and learned. Among them were "Ask Jesus to come into your heart," "Accept Jesus Christ as your personal savior," "We preach Christ crucified," and "Christ died once and for all." I found these phrases provocative, and I tried to learn what they meant. What does it mean, Jesus coming into your heart? What is a personal savior, and why "personal"? Was there another kind of savior besides "personal"? What does it mean, God loves you? What does "Jesus died for your sins" mean? What does it mean to be forgiven? Who am I and what am I supposed to do when I grow up? Who is God, anyway? And what does it mean that Jesus was his son? What does it mean to be saved? Saved from what?

I took these points of theology quite seriously, but I was puzzled by what they meant. If the church was throwing around words like "heaven," "hell," and "eternity," then these questions were of vital importance, I reasoned. There must be good, understandable answers.

Of all the questions about religion that began to plague me as an adolescent, the one I remember that really had me stumped occurred during Sunday School, when our teacher, who was also the student minister, asked us, "Why do we go to church every Sunday?" To praise God? someone suggested. But you can do that anywhere, said the student minister. To be with other Christians? You don't have to go to church on Sunday to do that, he said. To get re-charged, like a battery, I proposed. He just laughed. It seemed that every answer we offered was inadequate, and I really don't remember coming up with a good one.

I continued to go to church each week, but there seemed less and less reason to be there. We were assured that no matter what we did, we would be saved by faith, not by "works." We were made to feel especially nervous about signs of Phariseeism, of doing things in the hope that the action would somehow effect our salvation. In a Reformation backlash against Catholicism that was still burning after 400 years, we were taught that true religion occurred in your "heart" as opposed to your body. The things the body did -- hand and body gestures, reciting written prayers, handling beads, eating bread and wine -- were meaningless and even dangerous. There was a clear division made for us between body and soul, and the body and the soul could not participate together in worship. It was either one or the other, and God's way was in the heart and the head.

So for me the Sunday church service came to be little more than a chance to hear a more-or-less instructive sermon. It was Bible study with some hymns and prayers. Fortunately, our minister was a charismatic, brilliant man, and we did learn a great deal about the Bible. But his successor, who stepped in when I was in high school, just couldn't match his predecessor's skill as a preacher. I couldn't bear to listen to his sermons, which seemed to me silly at best, self-righteous and laden with anti-Catholic prejudice at worst. There didn't seem to be much reason to go to church when the sermons were poor because the sermon was the center of the service. And there was a certain amount of irony in that discovery, because we had been taught that as Protestants we could confess our sins directly to God, unlike the Catholics who, we were taught, could only reach God through a priest. I realized that in a Protestant worship service, where the sermon is central, if the minister is unintelligent or mean spirited it poisons everything in the service: the prayers, the singing, and certainly the sermon. At least Catholics had their Mass and their Eucharist, which remained the same regardless of the temperament of the priest. But I had been raised in an atmosphere so thoroughly anti-Catholic and opposed to any sort of ritual (the phrase was always "empty ritual," as though there were no other kind) that leaving the Reformed Church to become Catholic was something that didn't even occur to me. I just lost interest.

It wasn't that the Reformed Church was unable to justify itself adequately to me. I felt no anger toward the church, no deep disappointment. I think that if that had been the case I simply would have given up going to church, period. It was that the Reformed Church, God bless it, had made me aware of the Important Questions in life and instilled in me a deep hunger to answer those questions. That the Reformed Church's own answers did not satisfy me didn't matter all that much. I was grateful to have been set on a spiritual journey, grateful to have been taught how to pray, happy to have memorized so many Bible verses, and the books of the Bible and the Ten Commandments. I figured I had been well-prepared, and I was ready to move on.

Then I had a vision. In retrospect I call it a vision because I truly believe that God sent it to me for a reason, that it was some supernatural interference intended to add something to my thought pool. It happened on a warm, beautiful spring afternoon. I was coming home from high school, the last lone student on the school bus. I stepped off the bus at my stop, a street corner in an altogether ordinary suburban New Jersey setting, and as the bus pulled away I felt something strange. It was as though I could feel the world as a globe, and I could feel it turning around. I sensed that I was a figure on that globe. I stood still and felt the steady movement of the world, around and around. It was as though I were at the uppermost point, a sort of pole, and the world was turning around on the axis on which I stood. It was such a real feeling that I had to steady myself to keep from falling over. Then I slowly turned around on my axis and gazed at what was visible from where I stood: the four houses on the four corners of the crossroads, the tall pine trees in all the front yards, the mailboxes. And I realized that there was nobody in the whole world who could see what I was seeing from my great height: not even famous people, not even the President or the Beatles, not even terribly rich people. It wasn't that my view was so special, but I suddenly knew that it was entirely unique.

I remember going home and telling my mother, "Mom, I just felt like I was my own North Pole!" I could understand the vision no further than that at the time. But it has remained a fountain of understanding for me. The older I grew the more it revealed to me about myself, about other people, about God. I can say that this vision is the most important thing that happened to me in my life, and I am certain that it was a gift from God who could see that I needed something very big very fast.

In time I might have dismissed the vision as simply odd and adolescent, but I began reading about other people who have had the same experience. It's been like finding out that other people have dreams about missing final exams, when you thought you were the only one. Not all these people were led into the Orthodox Church because of it, however.

I stayed in the Reformed Church and even went to a Reformed Church college, Hope College, in Holland, Michigan. I must say that Hope is an excellent school; I say that even now. It isn't like some church-related colleges that are related in name only, with no apparent religious connection affecting campus life. Neither is it a protective, xenophobic place where professors are all required to be members of the school's denomination and students must sign conduct pledges. Chapel attendance at Hope was mandatory, and we had to take courses in Old and New Testament and a Senior Bible elective. But college life was exciting, vibrant and full. The first Catholic intellectual I ever met was my Chaucer professor at Hope. As she explained what Chaucer's England must have been like, and what the English language he spoke was like, we learned what the world must have been like before the Reformation.

I remember one anecdote she left with us: the word *free*, which to us today means the liberty to do whatever we please within limits without anybody telling us what to do, did not have that meaning hundreds of years ago. Free, she said, once meant "dear to the chief." That is, it was a way of describing a feudal relationship. You were either free or you were a serf. You performed your duties either because there was a special bond of affection between you and your lord, or because you had economic ties with your lord which necessitated that you perform certain functions. The first relationship, that of the free man, involved commitment and love; the second was strictly survival. The ancient meaning of freedom implied dependence, commitment, and love; it never happened in isolation.[1]

---

1   Later in graduate school I did a language exercise on the word *free*. After studying it in the Oxford English Dictionary I discovered that the ancient and original Indo-European word which gave birth to *free* must have meant love or beloved. From this source, all sorts of cousin-words were born which still exist in different languages: words for love, beloved, dear, and friend. The English word

by Nancy Forest-Flier

This was a powerful bit of news for me. It challenged two basic truths of Calvinism: that our salvation is a matter of predestination and not free will, and that we are saved on an individual basis. "The truth shall make you free," I had learned. Freedom was an aspect of the Kingdom of God. But whereas I had understood this freedom to apply to myself alone as a saved person, this new idea of freedom implied that others were involved, that there was some kind of loving dynamism that took place in salvation.

This would have been simply an interesting academic exercise for me if it hadn't been for that polar vision on the bus stop years before. I had been carrying the vision around with me since high school and it was still full of mystery. I was somehow convinced that that vision held an enormous truth, and I was determined to discover what it was. In the years after the vision happened, every time I considered it, the unavoidable facts struck me: each one of us is ultimately alone, no matter who he is; and each person's view of things is utterly unique. The challenge of *free* was that it seemed to fly in the face of facts: we are *not* ultimately alone. What could it mean?

When I thought about the vision at night, while lying by myself in the dark, it showed me its darkest, most frightening revelations: no matter how many friends we are able to gather around us, we are each going to die alone, we each must pass out of life entirely alone. And another: that each one of us has a unique view of the world and no two views are alike. It simply isn't possible for two people to have entirely similar and compatible understandings of anything. This kind of thinking was dismal and depressing, but it was real, I felt, and it was true. I began to see that everything that entered my consciousness through my senses was unique and colored by who I was, where I had been, and what kinds of events, both planned and accidental, happened around me. I remember saying to myself, "I'm not learning history, I'm learning Nancy's history; I'm not learning mathematics, I'm learning Nancy's mathematics." It would have led me to give up learning altogether if I wasn't certain that every student -- every person -- who ever lived hadn't existed in the same predicament. The possibility of real human contact seemed so bleak, so utterly preposterous.

---

friend is a sister word of *free*.

Then I was introduced to another literary figure with a bit more information, the American poet Wallace Stevens. Wallace Stevens was a contemporary of Robert Frost, Carl Sandburg and William Carlos Williams. I remember a particular afternoon sitting in the library with a friend. I had chosen Stevens's poetry as a term-paper topic, even though I knew almost nothing about his work. I opened my copy of his *Collected Poems* and began to read.

The first poem I read was the first in the book, "Earthy Anecdote." It was short and simple, describing a scene of a cat around whom a herd of bucks were forced to run. The poem described the bucks "clattering, /......../ in a swift, circular line / To the right, / Because of the firecat." It was an odd, simple poem, and somehow it reminded me of my polar vision: the cat sitting still and everything else being forced to revolve around it "in a swift circular line."[2] I kept thumbing through the book and came to "Anecdote of the Jar."

> *I placed a jar in Tennessee,*
> *And round it was, upon a hill.*
> *It made the slovenly wilderness*
> *Surround that hill.*
>
> *The wilderness rose up to it,*
> *And sprawled around, no longer wild.*
> *The jar was round upon the ground*
> *And tall and of a port in air.*
>
> *It took dominion everywhere.*
> *The jar was gray and bare.*
> *It did not give of bird or bush,*
> *Like nothing else in Tennessee.*[3]

When I read that poem I sat up in my chair. This man knew what my vision was all about! The lone individual (here a jar) with the random universe around it. But to Stevens, although the individual is indeed unique and alone ("Like nothing else in Tennessee"), because it just sits there within its circular vision and can take in everything around it, everything around it is "no longer wild"; everything begins to make sense.

---

2   Wallace Stevens, *The Collected Poems of Wallace Stevens* (New York, Alfred A. Knopf, 1969, p. 3)
3   *Ibid.*, p. 76.

By this time I was making not-very-quiet exclamations in the library and my friend was threatening to leave. In the following weeks I read many more of Stevens's poems. For a term-paper I decided to write about his long poem, "The Man with the Blue Guitar." That was more than twenty years ago, and I've forgotten whatever analysis I chose to pursue at the time. But I still recall that Stevens knew the polar vision, and he wrote about it. Stevens understood that each person is alone, each is unique and quite incapable of having more than a fragmented grasp of the world. But to each poor person, that jumbled mass of accidental things and events going on around him has a beauty, an organized, stunning beauty. There seems to be a sort of dynamic going on between the person standing there on his Pole and the world around him. He describes the Man with his Guitar:

> *He held the world upon his nose*
> *And this-a-way he gave a fling.*
> *His robes and symbols, ai-yi-yi–*
> *And that-a-way he twirled the thing.*
>
> *Sombre as fir-trees, liquid cats*
> *Moved in the grass without a sound.*
>
> *They did not know the grass went round.*[4]

Now the opposition between my insulated, isolated polar experience and the exciting truth about *free* with its give-and-take began to weaken a bit. We may be utterly alone, but we are in constant intercourse with the world around us; we make sense of it; we call it "beauty."

The theology in all this was not clear to me then. It's still only hazy to me now. But what is clear is that my spiritual journey, which had started with a few questions in Sunday School, had taken me to Wallace Stevens's door.

I needed to return to church. Somehow the connection between existential questions and church had been firmly planted in me. I needed to be in a fertile place where the deepest questions about the most basic human condition were at home, were ordinary table-talk. And because my vision had been such a physical one, I was desperate for a way of worshipping that was physical as well as intellectual. I wanted liturgy.

---

4   *Ibid.*, p. 178.

In the timid way in which many American Protestants make their move to a more liturgical kind of worship, I became an Episcopalian in my last year of college. The young priest at the local church was eager to help. In the Episcopal Church everything seemed optional, which was a good way for me to take up with liturgy for the first time. You could genuflect or not, cross yourself or not; the degree of "high church" that you adopted was up to you.

It was the form of the liturgy that attracted me. The beauty of the *Book of Common Prayer* appealed to my sense of English history, the way Chaucer and Spenser and Shakespeare did. It was stately English. And the words of the prayers could in no way be twisted or blunted by the state of mind of the priest.

My polar vision had taught me that one peculiarity of the human condition was the unique and fragmented viewpoint of each individual, no matter how intelligent. Somehow, having the words of worship all written down in a Book of Prayer elevated the worship, took it out of the hands of insufficient people, gave it a universality that was more trustworthy because it was not one single viewpoint. The Prayer Book, of course, was written by people, but there was something long-lasting and proven about it.

I did not become a deeply committed Episcopalian. I graduated from college and attended graduate school for one semester. Then I ran out of money, and I went home to New Jersey and hastily got myself married to a very young man who did not understand my spiritual struggle and seemed to have no interest in the Big Questions that kept me awake at night. I was suddenly drifting, my future hopes up for grabs.

I took a secretarial job at a religious peace organization nearby, the Fellowship of Reconciliation. There I met a couple of people whose conversation soon revealed to me that the Big Questions were not just midnight snacks for neurotics. Tom Cornell and Jim Forest were the only Catholics on the staff of the mostly-Protestant FOR. They had been active all their adult lives in the social justice wing of Catholicism. Both of them had worked at the Catholic Worker with Dorothy Day. Both were close friends with people, some of them priests, whose outspoken avowal of nonviolence and readiness to go to prison had made the headlines during the Vietnam War.

Jim Forest told me about Thomas Merton, a Trappist monk and friend of his who had died in 1968. Merton had been a convert to

by Nancy Forest-Flier

Catholicism. After entering the monastery of Our Lady of Gethsemani in Kentucky he continued a life of writing. The body of his work, including journals, essays, and poems, is enormous. At Jim's suggestion I read Merton's autobiography, Seven Storey Mountain, and it excited me. It wasn't the string of pious platitudes I had come to expect from "Christian" autobiographies (most of the writing I had been exposed to in this genre was the evangelical Protestant variety, usually involving the sudden and miraculous conversion of a Mafia thug or a Skid Row prostitute). Merton had been a bright, modern, cosmopolitan intellectual who had been hounded by the Big Questions until he had no choice but to pay very close attention to them.

I read more of Merton's writings. What fascinated me were his explanations (in many forms, essays and poems) of one's true identity, of who a person really is deep inside, in the center. My pondering over the polar vision kept me thinking about this very problem. If I stand on some kind of pole, with longitudinal lines emanating from me and encircling the globe, then those lines must start at some very central point within me. That which is not-me is everything outside that minute central point: my body, my clothing, my surroundings. I must have discovered the existence of my own soul. I must have realized that even when I die, when the not-me is lifeless and gone, that brilliant, living center of light will keep on living.

But what was it? Was it just some little essential version of me? I remembered turning around and around, seeing the suburban homes and the pine trees. Was everything in my life simply there by accident, for me to pick and choose from, or to swallow as gracefully as I could? Was every idea that I grabbed for to explain all this random stuff just that -- a convenient idea? Was God no more than a convenient idea? And Jesus? And the whole body of Christian dogma? Could I just shrug if it bored me and turn back to my pure, solitary self?

I began to see myself as a kind of onion with layer upon layer of tissue enclosing not very much at the center. I read in *Merton's New Seeds of Contemplation*:

> *All sin starts from the assumption that my false*
> *self, the self that exists only in my own egocentric*
> *desires, is the fundamental reality of life to which*
> *everything else in the universe is ordered. Thus I*
> *use up my life in the desire for pleasures and the*

> *thirst for experiences, for power, honor, knowl-*
> *edge and love, to clothe this false self and con-*
> *struct its nothingness into something objectively*
> *real. And I wind experiences around myself and*
> *cover myself with pleasures and glory like ban-*
> *dages in order to make myself perceptible to my-*
> *self and to the world, as if I were an invisible body*
> *that could only become visible when something*
> *visible covered its surface.*
>
> *But there is no substance under the things with*
> *which I am clothed. I am hollow, and my structure*
> *of pleasures and ambitions has no foundation. I*
> *am objectified in them. But they are all destined*
> *by their very contingency to be destroyed. And*
> *when they are gone there will be nothing left of me*
> *but my own nakedness and emptiness and hollow-*
> *ness, to tell me that I am my own mistake.*
>
> *The secret of my identity is hidden in the love and*
> *mercy of God.*[5]

Merton wrote that at one's very center is God himself, who "utters me like a word containing a partial thought of Himself." This was a great awakening for me. In all my years as a church-going Christian, I had never thought of God as something literally "within" me. Now, with this realization, the still-unanswered questions from my childhood, the polar vision on the bus stop, and the puzzle of *freedom* all seemed to come together. We are not alone. We are never alone; we cannot be. And "God" is not something "out there," something we first affirm and believe in, the product of our thought. The first act is God's within us. God "utters us." We are couched, cradled within his mercy.

To be free is to assent to God who is the deepest, truest, most central part of us. It is, as my Chaucer professor had told us, to be "dear to the chief," to be loved by God and in turn freely to give one's devotion to God. I kept thinking of the bus stop, of what it *felt* like to stand there and feel so central and alone. The North Pole. All lines of longitude emanating from your feet, crossing each other at one single point at your very center.

---

5   Thomas Merton, *New Seeds of Contemplation* (New York: New Directions Books, 1961, pp. 34-35)

And at that single point, at your very center, is where God, deep inside you, evokes life in you, generates an endless spring of love and mercy for you.

Finally I knew that what had happened to me on that bus stop was a vision indeed: it was God's way of showing me what it felt like to be free, to be loved and touched by grace. I knew that this experience was something I could hold up to every experience of worship I could have, that it would help guide me to a way of worshipping that was true.

I realized that most people, most of the time, don't choose to stand at that center point. Although it's hard to avoid being where you are physically, most people most of the time want to be elsewhere. Most people imagine that life would be better and they would be happier if only they were *out there* somewhere, not at the top of the world, not on this lonely North Pole. If only they were wealthier, healthier, better looking, married to someone else, someone else's child, living somewhere else, better educated, more confident, more graceful, more self-assertive; if only it were yesterday, or tomorrow, or in a few years when the children are grown; if only there were a different government, or a different president, or a different social system. *Then* life would be wonderful; it would be Paradise; it would be "Heaven."

For me, as a teenager and young adult, the temptations were certainly there. I had struggled with severe acne for many years. I tended to be lonely and painfully shy. My parents were classic non-communicators, unable to talk to me about problems or pain. If only, I thought. If only I were prettier. If only I were more self-confident. If only my parents were more open to me and more helpful. If only I had been born years earlier so that I wasn't one of the Baby Boomers who were glutting the graduate schools and deflating the value of graduate degrees. The blinding truth of that bus stop experience was all the more startling because of the desperation with which I longed to be different. But, the polar vision had taught me, the Kingdom of God is here right now, within you. To wish to be elsewhere is sin; it is slavery to a false hope. There is no freedom in it.

This heady stuff came at me all at once. I tried to share it with my husband, but he didn't seem interested and couldn't quite understand what the big deal was all about. Realizing that Merton had been a Catholic, I began attending a local Catholic church and started an instruction class with the church's priest. The priest was not a terribly bright teacher, and he had many of his facts wrong (especially those about Protestantism), but I was so convinced of the truth of Catholicism that I was willing to dismiss his mistakes. I was received into the Catholic church in 1979.

What I didn't realize at the time, and what I can see now, is that I was looking for the right way to worship. I was looking for Orthodoxy, which literally means the right way to give praise. But I didn't know anything about Orthodoxy at the time. I had never met an Orthodox Christian, knew absolutely nothing about the Orthodox Church. I had heard of Greek and Russian Orthodoxy, but I figured these were exotic and oriental forms of Christianity that could only be appreciated by Greeks and Russians. In truth, I never gave Orthodoxy a thought.

But now I can see a fairly direct line between the polar vision on the bus stop and my entry into the Catholic church. God had arrested my attention in a startling, physical way. I wanted to meet God again in the same way, in a physical way, standing so that the things around me were organized around me, not tempting me with other flashy false centers that seemed like another, better reality. When I took Communion in the Catholic church, it was an affirmation of God's life within me. Yes, the church said, God is really deep inside you. In his extraordinary mercy and humility and love, God takes up residence inside.

And this is how I began to learn about the Mother of God. Mary is nothing more than an historical figure in Calvinist teaching, and I was always deeply suspicious of the Catholic regard for Mary when I was a child. Yet the Mary I came to love became real to me when I realized that we are all God-bearers, but deeply, mortally flawed. Mary bore God in a profound, physical way and with perfect obedience.

I attended the local Catholic church faithfully, although I found the worship a bit cloying. I went to receive Communion. This was the single link with the polar vision that I held fast to each Sunday. I tried to ignore the music, which I found distracting. It seemed like an unsuccessful attempt to be modern, relevant, to get people's attention. The songs the choir sang from "Godspell," and the other contemporary religious music, were jarring to me. The hymns that the jolly deacon encouraged everybody to sing were silly and embarrassing.

At this point I changed jobs, leaving the Fellowship of Reconciliation, where I had worked on the organization's magazine staff as typesetter, to take a position in a small graphics and typesetting shop in a nearby town. Typesetting fascinated me, and I wanted to really learn the craft completely. The shop was owned by an Orthodox Jewish family. It was my first encounter with orthodoxy of any kind, and I must say that the extent of my appreciation of Orthodox Judaism had a great deal to do with my eventually becoming an Orthodox Christian. I had never met a family like this before: their religion touched and affected almost every aspect of their lives. Their fasting, their feasting, the mezuzahs fixed to the doorways throughout the shop, everything seemed to float on an undercurrent of faith, seemed to be rinsed and sweetened by faith. I made friends with the couple and they showed me their kosher kitchen, told me about Jewish holidays and beliefs. I began to yearn for that kind of faith: a serious faith that wasn't timid about advancing into every corner of your life and laying claim to it. But I didn't know of any sort of Christianity, except for some groups like the Amish, which did this.

So I continued to attend the Catholic church. About two years after I became a Catholic, my marriage fell apart. It died of an absence of care and respect, it died of immaturity and selfishness, of hopelessly divergent interests. There was one child from that marriage, Caitlan, a little girl then five years old. And in one of those crazy twists that life sometimes takes, in a story that a fiction-writer would never touch because it sounds so improbable, I ended up marrying my old friend Jim Forest who had first told me about Thomas Merton.

Jim was in Europe at the time, in the Netherlands, where he had been living for five years. We had been keeping up a friendly correspondence, writing about books we were reading and about our spiritual journeys. His own marriage had disintegrated. Finally at the end of 1981 we decided to marry. So on Easter Monday in 1982, Caitlan and I boarded a KLM flight to Amsterdam and we moved to Jim's house in Alkmaar, where we have been living ever since.

It was extraordinary living with someone with whom I could pray. It hardly seemed possible, after living for so many years in a spiritually empty marriage. I was eager to begin sharing my spiritual journey with Jim and I began attending church with him. This was the start of a valiant search for a church-home in Holland, during which time we learned a great deal about the state of Christianity in western Europe.

My polar vision was tucked neatly into my heart, still as warm and alive as the day it happened. It had grown up a bit; it was incubating and maturing. It had been enriched by Thomas Merton and Catholicism and my Orthodox Jewish friends. I still regarded it as the spiritual yardstick against which I could measure my attempts at worship.

At first, I accompanied Jim to the Catholic church he attended, Pius X. It was a modern building in a new section of Alkmaar, and it was filled every Sunday with young families. The church had two large children's choirs, one for youngsters and one for teenagers. It had an active group of lay parishioners who worked hard to make each Mass interesting and relevant to current social problems. The songbook we sang from consisted of popular melodies with Dutch texts, most of them faintly religious with a strong slant toward active social concern. The things I had become familiar with in the American Catholic church were absent there: the holy water fonts were dry, there were no kneelers and no kneeling, the Host was kept in an inconspicuous side chapel, there were no confessionals and no evidence of confession. And Mass was quite different, too. Every aspect of the service was meant to encourage active concern for the Third World, the poor, guest workers, the handicapped, minorities. It was an admirable effort, but for me it had little to do with real worship and communion. The unspoken basis for the church's direction seemed to be a belief that in order for justice to be done in the world, it had to be specifically fostered during Mass; the dark side of this was a fear that a purely "religious" Mass by its very nature neglected the need for justice.

We decided to switch churches, so we began attending a church near our house right across the canal. We went faithfully to St. Joseph's for almost two years. It was a much more traditional place, with much of the Mass still in Latin and a less experimental approach to worship. But there were no young families in the congregation, no children. It seemed to be a gathering place for older Catholics whose obligation-minded practice of Mass-attendance had been formed well before the Second Vatican Council. No one ever spoke to us. After awhile we left to continue our search.

At St. Laurence Church the Masses were more of the same, so we decided to join the choir. At least, we thought, we might feel some sense of acceptance, feel some proximity to the "action," if we were actually closer to the altar and singing the Mass. We were clearly the youngest people in the choir, and during the choir practice coffee break we listened to the older members talk nostalgically about the "old days" when the fasts were kept and people went to confession.

by Nancy Forest-Flier

I hesitate to use our limited experience of church-searching to evaluate the state of Christianity in western Europe, but I'm not encouraged by anything else I've seen. Last Easter we listened to a program on the BBC in which it was revealed that some 60% of Britons responding to a poll didn't know what event Easter was supposed to be celebrating. A friend of ours, a Dutch Catholic priest who lived and taught in the United States for many years, returned to his home in the south of the Netherlands for a family visit and went to see an old priest there who was known as a great confessor years ago. Our friend asked the old priest to hear his confession. The old priest was deeply touched and said, "You know, no one has come to me for confession in seven years." Another friend, who lives here and is active in Pax Christi, wanted to organize a staff retreat for contemplation, recollection, and spiritual renewal. The retreat was finally planned, but the rest of the staff insisted that it be organized around "relevant topics" such as hunger and oppression in the Third World or inclusive language in the liturgy. No one wanted to come together for prayer.

In the meantime, people are suffering from a kind of spiritual anemia which cannot be touched by broad programs for social development or progressive ideology. The state of the parish Catholic church was so deeply disturbing that we didn't really know where to turn. Our older children (Jim had three children by his former marriage who all lived nearby in Alkmaar) had soured on church entirely. Then something happened that signaled the beginning of a new life for us: Jim had a sabbatical coming up and we decided to spend it in Jerusalem. He was asked by the Ecumenical Institute at Tantur, situated on the road between Jerusalem and Bethlehem, to teach a three-month course in peacemaking. We were able to go as a family, which meant both Caitlan, then eight years old, and our youngest child, Anne, who was less than two at the time.

It was in Jerusalem that I first encountered Orthodoxy. It was extraordinarily exotic to me at first, all those icons and incense and chanting, all those monks in black with their various kinds of headdress. I never made many inquiries into Orthodoxy while I was in Jerusalem. I just took in the outward impressions. We visited the monastery of Mar Saba in the Jordan valley where, I later learned, St. John of Damascus took refuge. I saw the hermits' caves peppering the cliffsides in the wilderness. We were befriended by a leader from Jerusalem's Armenian community and attended a liturgy in the beautiful, ancient Orthodox church of St. James. But I also visited many Catholic churches that were spiritually powerful places. One of my favorites was the Church of St. Anne.

At the end of our stay in Jerusalem we rented a car and drove around Galilee, visiting all the holy places around Lake Tiberias. One afternoon our route took us to Mount Tabor, the site of the Transfiguration. We drove up the steep, narrow road to the church at the top of the mountain, parked, and went inside. Like so many of the churches built on the holy sites, this one was awesome in its dimensions and decoration. But one interesting aspect of this particular church caught my attention: a round circle laid in the stonework floor in the center of the church, with an X transecting it. I went up to this circle and stood in the center of the X, and suddenly it happened again: the polar vision, the unmistakable brush with pure reality. Only this time I found myself standing not on my New Jersey bus stop but on the Pole of Poles: the place where the Lord himself had been transfigured before his disciples.

Of course, the X had been laid in the floor to indicate the place of the Transfiguration. But when I stood there myself and the whole earth fell away from me on all sides, I was able to draw some unavoidable conclusions: that as Merton had said, the very center of the human individual is God, and that we are so confused and distracted by sin that we are almost never able to be there, where we should be, where we are truly ourselves, where God is. If that were possible, we would be transfigured, too. We would shine like the sun.

Shaken, I joined the rest of the family and we left the church.

I left Israel with little more interest in Orthodoxy than when we had arrived, but among the items we carried back to Holland with us was our first icon. Jim had spotted it in one of those little shops inside the Jaffa Gate in the Old City. It was quite small, a hand-painted icon of the Mother of God with the child Jesus in her arms, and it was almost hidden amidst all the other bits of antiquity, coffee urns, and jewelry displayed in the shop window. The owner, whose bottle of Jack Daniels was already open by 10:00 a.m. and whose interest in the real value of the things in his shop was minimal, said he'd sell it to us for $100. For us $100 was a considerable amount of money, so we let the icon sit in the shop while we went back to our apartment at the Institute to think it over. It was more than just a souvenir, but what it was and why it seemed to have attached itself to us was mysterious. Finally we decided to buy it. We brought it back and set it on our apartment book-shelf. A Melchite priest we had met at the Institute examined the icon and guessed it had been brought to Jerusalem by a 19th-century Russian pilgrim.

We brought the icon home with us and hung it over the mantle. Then we set a little oil lamp in front of it. Then we began praying together before it, using all sorts of prayers: Catholic prayers from our breviaries, Jewish prayers from a Jewish prayerbook we had picked up in Jerusalem. We set other icons around our Mother of God: a copy of the Rublev Holy Trinity, given to us by a friend as a wedding present. A tiny icon of Joachim and Anne embracing each other which we had bought from the Little Sisters of Jesus on the Via Dolorosa. There were other things that we arranged on the mantle around the oil lamp: some acorns from the Oak of Mamre in Hebron, the old Dutch family Bible that my great-grandparents had brought with them when they emigrated from Holland to America. Our "icon corner" was taking shape, and we weren't even Orthodox yet!

But it wasn't long. Jim, who was working as the General Secretary of the International Fellowship of Reconciliation, had developed a strong interest in the Russian Orthodox Church after having visited Moscow with religious and peace movement representatives. He began working on his first book about the Russian Church and was invited to visit the USSR and begin research. He made several trips to work on the book, and each time he brought home dozens of books and stories about Orthodox fasting and prayer, about the Liturgy, about the powerful spirituality he found in Russian churches.

In the summer of 1987 I was able to accompany Jim on a two-week trip to Moscow, Smolensk, Minsk, and Brest. Finally, I was to attend a Russian Orthodox Liturgy myself. On the first Sunday we were in Moscow and, being careful to dress appropriately and cover my head, I walked with Jim up the steps of the church of Our Lady of Tikhvin. Beggars lined the outer steps, extending their hands, and parishioners carefully placed money in the outstretched palms. I felt as though I had been transplanted into a Dostoevsky novel.

We went inside. It was a small church, and there weren't very many people there that day. An old nun dressed in black from head to foot was standing at the front of the church, attending the candles that were being placed before the icons. A young mother came in with her little girl and stood in front of us. When the little girl became restless from standing, the old nun offered her a little chair. But the child just clung to her mother's legs and finally sat on the floor next to her. How wonderful, I thought, that children can just sit on the floor here.

Someone tapped me on the shoulder, and when I turned around the woman behind me handed me a piece of paper. Jim told me to give it to the old nun, which I did, and she in turn gave it to a deacon. Later I learned that it had prayer requests written on it for the priest to read off during the Liturgy.

I don't remember much about the Liturgy because I didn't understand it at all and I had no groundings. But I do recall the spiritual atmosphere in that church, the intense, serious, profound power that wrapped itself around me. There were no silly religious songs or frivolous attempts to keep the parishioners interested. There seemed to be a basic difference between this kind of worship and all the rest I had ever known: the services in the west were like religious presentations in which the clergy, with or without a "worship committee," would put together a service with songs and readings and sermons, hoping to keep the people's attention. It was common to walk out of a church saying, "That was a great Mass!" It was almost like entertainment, like a show. All the action was done by certain actors: the priest or minister, the choir, the readers.

You sat in your place and watched. But in that Orthodox church, I felt that every person had a role to play, parishioner and priest alike. There didn't seem to be an attempt to keep people's attention by trying to be "relevant" or "amusing." Once you stepped into the church you were part of a great drama, you stood and acted out your part. You kissed icons, lit candles, bowed, prostrated yourself, crossed yourself. The act of worship suddenly became comprehensible to me. That old question from my Reformed Church Sunday School, "Why do we go to church?" was answered in the Orthodox Liturgy. Because this truly was an *act* of worship; it was everyone involved in a drama.

There were many visits to Orthodox churches during those two weeks. During one visit I remember going into a church at a time when a Liturgy was not occurring. We walked around the interior with the member of the church council as he told us about the icons and the history of the church. Then, finding myself in the center of the church, I happened to look directly over me and saw a great icon overhead: Christ in glory, painted within a vast circle. As I stood there, trying to understand this amazing place, I was reminded of the church on the Mount of the Transfiguration. Right in the center: Christ himself. And it all clicked: this place was made for worship. I turned slowly around, as I had turned around on that sunny afternoon on the New Jersey bus stop. But instead of pine trees and suburban houses, there were icons of the saints. Some of the saints I knew, many I didn't, but they all stood there, solemnly facing me.

I knew nothing about icons then. I didn't know what they meant, how they fit into the Orthodox theological framework. I didn't know the history of iconography or the stories of certain great iconographers. I didn't know how icons are "written," or how the icon painter has to prepare himself. All I knew was that Christ was with me as I stood there at the top of the world, and all the saints stood around me. It was not the "slovenly wilderness" that Wallace Stevens had sensed with his lonely jar on the hill. It was a universe made beautiful not by the beholder but by God, whose love carried forth in the lives of the saints and been witnessed to for centuries in the life of the church. (I learned some time later that Wallace Stevens, about whom I knew very little, had become a Catholic on his deathbed.)

The action during the Orthodox liturgy was not dependent on the charisma of the minister or the priest; it was the lively witness of all the saints, of each believer standing on his particular pole, of the priest and the deacons, of all the community in prayer together.

We returned home in the summer of 1987, both of us deeply affected by our time in the Russian churches. Then in January of 1988 Jim was invited to attend the opening celebration of the Millennium of Christianity in Russia. It was to be held at the Russian Orthodox Church of St. Nicolas of Myra in Amsterdam. We both decided to go, wondering if the intense spiritual power of the churches of Russia could ever find a mirror in the spiritually impoverished west.

It was not a Liturgy, but there was music and prayers. We stood in the tiny chapel that served as the Russian Orthodox Church. It was crowded with parishioners and guests and representatives of all the Christian communities in the area. Afterward we went to the parish house for a social time, and much to our astonishment, members of the parish came up to us, greeted us, expressed interest in who we were, and invited us to return. It was the first time any Dutch church had been so kind and hospitable to us.

We decided to attend a Liturgy, which was quite an undertaking since we live about 25 miles from Amsterdam and have no car. But the train system in Holland is superb, and we found that the trip by train and tram was quite simple.

We brought Anne with us. The older children had been so turned off by church that it was quite impossible to talk them into coming along. (We still pray that some day they may be willing to join us.) To our astonishment and joy, the Liturgy was just as powerful and beautiful as we had found it in Russia. We decided to try to return every other week (we were still singing in the choir at our local Catholic church). But after one week back at the Catholic church, which seemed like thin soup compared to the rich feast of Orthodoxy, we realized we had to make a break. We left the Catholic church choir and began the weekly trek into Amsterdam, which we've been doing now for more than four years.

That was in January, 1988. On Palm Sunday Jim was received into the Orthodox Church. I needed a bit more time, but not much. I was received on Pentecost.

I am aware that it is a Protestant habit to evaluate one's choices and experiences from a purely individual standpoint, and that I am in danger of evaluating my journey to Orthodoxy in a Protestant way. In other words, I can look at my journey as a slow working out of a unique experience which happened to me, with my "discovery" of Orthodoxy as the resolution of it all. There is the danger that I might use my own rather primitive experience to validate the Orthodox Church, to say "It feels right to me, so it must be true."

I admit that at first this was true. The Orthodox Church felt right to me because I could lay my own experience over it and everything seemed to line up. I think the basic truth of my polar experience was that we can only see and judge everything from our own extremely limited situation, and therefore we run the risk of putting everything -- even God and the Church -- together into the collection of things "out there" along with the pine trees and suburban houses. But somehow (and this is the mysterious part of it all) God used this experience to lead me into a new kind of understanding. Although I may stand at this dizzying height (and for me it was dizzying indeed), under the impression that everything is subject to my whim and judgment, it is God who is at the center. And I must struggle to unite myself with God who is the center of my self, and so to continue viewing the world around me.

There have been many words coming to me to describe my journey so far, but few to adequately express where I am now. I am learning to listen and to pray. I am learning what it means to worship (the old Sunday School question about the reason for going to church is no longer so obscure). I am praying for humility, for a penitential spirit, for the spirit of forgiveness. And I am overcome by the knowledge that God in his mercy has shown me his home at the center of the world.

Orthodoxy: Jewish and Christian
by Fr. A. James Bernstein

I am a Jew by birth. Our family roots are in Jerusalem, near the Mount of Olives, where my four grandparents are buried.

My father, Isaac, was born in the old walled city of Jerusalem. He received his rabbinical certificate from the venerable chief rabbi of Jerusalem, Rabbi Yosef Chaim Sonnenfeld. My father, however, was not a rabbi for long. World War II and its slaughter of millions of Jews contributed to his loss of faith.

My parents had no choice as to whom they would marry, for while still children their marriage had been arranged by their parents. This was the tradition -- the way it had been for thousands of years among the ultra-Orthodox Jews. I'm not complaining, though; they produced me!

The family moved to Lansing, Michigan where I was born, and later to Queens, New York, where I was raised. One day in 1962, when I was sixteen years of age, a friend gave me a "forbidden" book -- the New Testament. I studied it in secret, under the covers in my bedroom at night, with a flashlight. As I read it, I felt both fear and guilt. Fear of what my father would do if he discovered me reading it and guilt for betraying my people and heritage. I felt as if my Jewish ancestors were crying out to me, "Traitor, you are betraying your people!" And the impossible happened. As I read the New Testament I began to believe it and felt compelled to follow Jesus Christ.

The life of Christ presented in the Bible moved me deeply. The New Testament seemed to me to be a natural continuation of the Old Testament. In Christ the age-old struggle between a loving God and an unbelieving people came to a dramatic head. Praying to God, I asked, "If Jesus is the Messiah, let it be shown me." Soon after, in an intensely personal, spiritual experience, I felt assured of His reality.

This encounter with God didn't involve visions, hearing voices, or witnessing anything spectacular. It was rather the experiencing of God as an overwhelming personal presence, as if a light had suddenly appeared in the darkness of my heart. Prior to this encounter, I often had questioned the reality of His existence. Now I experienced the reality of His presence in a way I never had before. This sense of the ever-presence of God would remain with me through the ensuing years of my life.

Being convinced of the truth of Christianity, I next began searching for a Christian church. Since I knew nothing about churches, I became what was easiest for me to become, an Independent (with a capital I) Protestant. This was "safe," for I could read the Bible and develop my own beliefs without being too committed to the Church. In fact, I didn't even have to join or be baptized. Best of all, I could disassociate myself from nominal denominational Churches. But this didn't mean I wanted to be anonymous. To the contrary, I wanted to go "all out" in my commitment to Jesus Christ. At Queens College in New York City, I became very active in a group called Inter-Varsity Christian Fellowship and became president. To maintain my Jewish identity, I also sought out and became attached to some Jewish-Christian fellowship groups.

After graduating from Queens College in 1970, I accompanied the Reverend Moishe Rosen and a few other Jewish-Christians to the West Coast in order to establish a brand new organization called "Jews for Jesus." The purpose of this Evangelical Protestant Mission to the Jews was to make known that there are Jews who believe in Jesus and continue to retain a Jewish heritage. In this effort the mission was extremely successful and it received widespread national and international media coverage. It eventually was to become the most active and effective Protestant mission to Jews in the world. I did not remain with Jews for Jesus for long. Though I agreed with much of what Jews for Jesus sought, it was fundamentally a para-church mission and I had begun my quest to discover "church" and community.

I moved to Berkeley, California and became active in the 70's Jesus Movement. Berkeley was the vortex of the challenging youth culture in America. The Evangelical Protestant ministry with which I now became active, "Christian World Liberation Front" and its associated house churches, sought to present Jesus to those in the counter-culture in ways to which they could relate. They did this by emphasizing the more radical aspects of Jesus's ministry and by emphasizing community.

My involvement in evangelical Protestantism was a positive experience. The churches usually had strong communities, were Bible-centered, and provided good preaching. But somehow I sensed a lack of worship. I missed the traditional Biblical Jewish emphasis upon worship that I had experienced as a young boy in the synagogue. Nevertheless, I hung in there and told myself, "no church is perfect."

Rediscovering the Place of Worship

As the years passed, my desire to experience worship as described in the Bible grew. It became increasingly clear to me as I studied Scripture that everything the prophets and Apostles did -- whether it was preaching, teaching, evangelism, good deeds, or fellowship -- was pervaded by praise and worship of God. The Bible states that immediately after Pentecost, the disciples were "continuing daily with one accord in the temple, and breaking bread from house to house, they ate their food with gladness and simplicity of heart, praising God and having favor with all the people" (*Acts 2: 46-47*).

From ancient times Christians gathered together to worship God, not as "fellowship groups" but around Holy Communion; not around a charismatic preacher but around the "breaking of bread," the Body and Blood of Christ.

As a Jewish-Christian, I came to realize it was not enough for me to accept the Jewish Messiah, Our Lord Jesus Christ. I also had to discover the Church that He began through the early Jewish converts. What became of the early Jewish-Christian Church in the book of Acts? Where could I find such a worship-centered church? I was tired of sitting in church asking myself, "Why am I here?" "Why don't I feel fed?" "When will this sermon end?" "Why doesn't this service feel spiritual?" "When are we going to stop talking about worship and do it?"

I finally decided to visit some churches that I had heard put the emphasis on worship. They were "spirit filled," charismatic-Pentecostal churches. I found enthusiasm and warmth there, but the worship generated more heat than light. It was not the worship I had seen in the Bible. It was far too dependent upon the abilities of individual leaders to entertain, too self-serving, often out of control.

There seemed no place left to go. I had checked out a wide variety of Protestant churches and none had that Biblically based Jewish-Christian worship I was looking for. I visited a few Catholic masses, including folk masses, but the services seemed too casual. Besides, I knew that there were serious theological disagreements between Protestantism and Catholicism. My friend, Jack Sparks, had been studying worship in the early

Church. We talked repeatedly. One day I decided to check out a church that I had never visited and knew little about. It was a church that claimed to worship based on the ancient Jewish-Christian patterns. I went somewhat warily to this Orthodox Christian church.

To my pleasant surprise, I immediately felt a distinct sense of being in the presence of God the moment I walked inside the church. It was like stepping back in time with Christ and entering the ancient Jewish Temple in Jerusalem! Everything about the service was centered in the worship of the Most High God.

The music was much different from what I was accustomed to hearing in Protestant churches. It was more subdued and had a mystical quality. The prayers used during the service were mostly from the Bible and were chanted very much like they are in the Jewish synagogue. Visually, the interior of the Church reminded me of the ancient Temple -- it was stunning. And there was an altar with a Jewish-looking candelabrum on it! Following the service, I went home and found the sweet aroma of the incense had pervaded my clothes. It was as if I had brought some of the heavenly presence home with me!

As a Protestant, I had forgotten how beautiful and spiritual Biblical temple worship was. I had begun to think of Temple worship as something corrupt and of beauty in worship as suspect. It was necessary to remind myself that Temple worship had been established not by man but by God, and that it was beautiful, indeed majestic.

The ancient temple, many believed, was built upon a foundation of white marble covered with gold. The entrance into the Holy Place had a golden door. Within the Holy Place were the golden candlesticks, the table of showbread, and the altar of incense. Outside the temple was an immense laver made of brass that was supported by twelve colossal bulls. The most prominent object in the court of the priests was the immense altar of unhewn stones. The high priest wore eight sacred vestments. The robe of ephod was adorned at the hem by alternate blossoms of colorful pomegranate and golden bells. His breast plate was encrusted with twelve jewels, each bearing a name of one of the twelve tribes.

The services in the ancient temple were mainly sung and chanted. Two choirs would sing the psalms antiphonally. The incense burned upon the altar consisted of four ingredients mentioned in the book of Exodus, as well as others that give off a dense smoke. During services different sets of priests had different tasks to do. Everything was done with great order, dignity, and pomp.

This form of worship included the use of incense, imagery, statuary, vestments, precious metals and stones, priestly orders, litanies, chants, bells and candles. All of this God had established; but I, as an evangelical Protestant, had come to believe it was at best inferior worship and at worst, corrupt worship.

Where Heaven and Earth Meet

I decided to study Orthodox Christianity more seriously. I discovered that in the Bible, whenever God revealed Himself to man, it was in a setting of worship that included beauty, order, and majesty. Both Old Testament and New Testament worship sought to reflect on earth the majesty of God as revealed from heaven.

The prophet Ezekiel had such an intense vision of God being worshipped in heaven that he had difficulty describing it in conventional terms. He speaks of a whirlwind, a great cloud with raging fire engulfing itself, lightning, an awesome crystal, the voice of an army, and a throne. He saw on the throne a being with the appearance of a man. He fell on his face in awe.

In a similar vein, I also discovered in the New Testament a reaffirmation of the heavenly majesty of God. Along with this reaffirmation is the dramatic revelation of the Father's grace and love to us in Christ. The writer of the book of Hebrews says, in contrasting the New Covenant with the Old Covenant: "But you have come to Mount Zion and to the city of the living God, the heavenly Jerusalem, to an innumerable company of angels, to the general assembly and Church of the firstborn who are registered in heaven, to God the Judge of all, to the spirits of just men made perfect, to Jesus the Mediator of the new covenant, and to the blood of sprinkling that speaks better things than that of Abel. See that you do not refuse Him who speaks" (*Hebrews 12: 22-25*). He concludes by saying, "For our God is a consuming fire."

In the last book of the Bible, a vision of Our Lord Jesus Christ enthroned and worshipped in heaven is described in which "His countenance was like the sun shining in its strength" (*Revelation, 1:16*). John speaks further of the throne as surrounded by twenty-four other thrones upon which twenty-four elders sit. There are four living creatures which

"...do not rest day or night, saying: 'Holy, holy, holy, Lord God Almighty, Who was, and is, and is to come!'" (*Revelation 4:8*).

The Scriptures were clearly saying to me that God is worshipped in great glory in heaven, with great solemnity and grandeur. His worship is awesome. Unfortunately, many modern Christians tend to think of God as a cosmic "buddy." This familiar view of God greatly undermines worship. God loves us and is in the deepest sense our friend. But He is the everlasting God, our Creator, King, and Judge. Even the Apostle John, who is described in the Gospels as "the beloved" of the Lord because of his closeness to Christ, "fell at His feet as though dead" upon seeing Christ enthroned in heaven. If this beloved apostle and friend of Christ fell at His feet in worship, how much more readily should we worship Him in the dignity of humility?

As a Jew I knew that God had established the ancient Temple in Jerusalem, with all its elaborate ritual, to give us a glimpse of that worship which is continuous in heaven. Moses had been instructed by God to make the tabernacle after the pattern of the heavenly prototype as seen in *Exodus 25: 9,40* "And let them make Me a sanctuary, that I may dwell among them. According to all that I show you, that is the pattern of the tabernacle and the pattern of all its furnishings, just so you shall make it.... And see to it that you make them according to the pattern which was shown you on the mountain." And later in *Hebrews 8:4-5*, "...there are priests who offer the gifts according to the law; who serve the copy and shadow of the heavenly things, as Moses was divinely entrusted when he was about to make the tabernacle. For he said, 'see that you make all things according to the pattern shown you on the mountain.'" This is the background in which the early Jewish-Christian Church understood worship: seeking to reflect the heavenly worship in their worship on earth.

I began to renew my research of Jewish-Christian worship. The first Christians, I knew, were Jews and familiar with both Temple and synagogue worship, but I discovered that in their worship they had included elements from both Temple and synagogue. The first portion of the Jewish-Christian service incorporated synagogue worship in its reading from the Torah and Prophets, its use of Psalms, hymnology and its use of teaching. As central elements of acts of worship, Protestant services have inherited the synagogue's use of Scripture reading and preaching.

But in the second part of the ancient service I discovered that the Jewish-Christians incorporated ancient Temple worship. This included priests as officiants of priestly worship, an offertory, and an *epiclesis* or calling down of the Holy Spirit upon the bread, wine, and the congregation. It also included a re-presenting of the sacrifice of Christ to God the Father and the communal eating of the sacrifice by those for whom the sacrifice had been offered.

Jewish worship was always physical and visual. The Old Testament people of God worshipped with music, with color, with light and candles, with sweet aroma and incense, with art, with rhythmic chant, with feasts and fasts, with cycles of holy days, and with godly order and liturgy. I came to realize these things were neither pagan in origin nor temporal in character. They were fulfilled in Christ and retained.

As I attended subsequent Orthodox services, it became clear that the Orthodox Church had inherited, kept, and practiced Biblical worship.

Orthodox Christian liturgy has inherited the same elements of Temple worship found in early Jewish-Christian services, which have been either de-emphasized or totally eliminated from evangelical Protestant worship. As I came to a fuller appreciation of Orthodox Christian liturgy, I began to see an even greater overlap with ancient Temple worship in very many details.

There is a temple/church, a priest, a sanctuary and an altar. Upon the altar is a seven branched candelabrum as in the ancient Temple. The priest says special prayers before coming to church and prior to entering the sanctuary so as to consecrate himself for service. This is as it was with the ancient priests.

> *You are the heads of the fathers' houses of the Levites. Sanctify yourselves, you and your brethren, that you may bring up the ark of the Lord God of Israel to the place I have prepared for it. For because you did not do it the first time, the Lord our God broke out against us, because we did not consult Him about the proper order. So the priests and the Levites sanctified themselves to bring up the ark of the Lord God of Israel.*
>
> *(I Chronicles 15:12-14)*

The Orthodox Christian priest then vests himself with various special items of cloth and says special prayers over each as each item represents a divine truth. He expresses his unworthiness for worship as he washes his hands before serving as the ancient Jewish priests did.

> *Then the Lord spoke to Moses saying: You shall also make a basin of bronze, with its base also of bronze, for washing. You shall put it between the tabernacle of meeting and the altar. And you shall put water in it, for Aaron and his sons shall wash their hands and their feet in water from it. When they go into the tabernacle of meeting, or when they come near the altar to minister, to burn an offering made by fire to the Lord, they shall wash with water, lest they die. So they shall wash their hands and feet, lest they die. And it shall be a requirement forever to them -- to him and his descendants throughout their generations.*
>
> *(Exodus 30: 17-21)*

> *Then Moses brought Aaron and his sons and washed them with water. And he put the tunic on him, girded him with the sash, clothed him with the robe, and put the ephod on him; and he girded him with the intricately woven band of the ephod, and with it tied the ephod on him. Then he put the breast plate on him and he put the Urim and the Thummim in the breastplate. And he put the turban on his head. Also on the mitre, on its front, he put the golden plate, the holy crown, as the Lord had commanded Moses.*
>
> *(Leviticus 8: 6-9)*

> *Now Solomon began to build the house of the Lord at Jerusalem on Mount Moriah.... He also made ten lavers ... the Great Basin was for the priests to wash in.*
>
> *(2 Chronicles 3: 4-6)*

Many candles, including the seven branched candelabrum which is upon the altar, whose beauty is reminiscent of the lamp-stands in Solomon's Temple, illuminate the sanctuary and nave of Orthodox churches.

Thus Solomon had all the furnishings made for the house of God: the altar of gold and the tables on which was the showbread; the lamp-stands with their lamps of pure gold, to burn in the prescribed manner in front of the inner sanctuary, with the flowers and the lamps and the wick-trimmers of gold; the trimmers, the bowls, the ladles, and the censers of pure gold. (*II Chronicles 4:19-22*) Special prayers are said by the Orthodox priest in preparing the bread, called the lamb, to be offered. The service then begins with everyone standing and facing the altar: east, as do the Jews. The priest raises his hands, as did the High Priest, and calls upon the Spirit of God to be present. Censing with incense forms an aromatic cloud, an image of God's presence, a reminder to us of how God's glory filled the consecrated Temple in Jerusalem.

> *And it came to pass, when the priests came out of*
> *the holy place, that the cloud filled the house of*
> *the Lord, so that the priests could not continue*
> *ministering because of the cloud; for the glory of*
> *the Lord filled the house of the Lord.*
> *(I Kings 8:10-11)*

Incense also reminds us of our prayers which rise as sweet aroma to God. Because of its deep spiritual imagery and because of its impact upon our senses, incense is used in both Temple worship and Orthodox Christian worship. The Lord said to Moses: "You shall make an altar to burn incense ... before the Lord throughout your generations" (*Exodus 30:1-8*). And Moses, "... made the incense altar of cacia wood ... and he overlaid it with pure gold.... He also made the holy anointing oil and the pure incense of sweet spices, according to the work of the perfumer" (*Exodus 37:28-29*).

The Orthodox Church has within it many icons which remind us that we are not only in God's presence as we worship, but also in the presence of His holy angels and of our brethren in Christ who have gone before us into glory. Unfortunately, as an evangelical Protestant, I had thought that the making and veneration of icons was idolatrous. Somehow I had forgotten that the making of certain images was commanded by God Himself in the Bible. It was not the making of all images that was prohibited, but the making of images to be worshipped as gods.

> *Moreover, you shall make the tabernacle with ten*
> *curtains woven of fine linen thread, and blue and*
> *purple and scarlet yarn; with artistic designs of*
> *cherubim you shall weave them.*   *(Exodus 26:1)*

> *Now king Solomon sent and brought Hiram from Tyre ... a bronze worker; he was filled with wisdom and understanding and skill in working with all kinds of bronze work. So he came to King Solomon and did all his work.... So he made the pillars, and two rows of pomegranates above the network all around to cover the capitals.... The tops of the pillars were in the shape of lilies.... Then he made the Basin of cast bronze... And below its brim were ornamental birds encircling it all around.... It stood on twelve oxen. He also made ten carts of bronze.... And this was the design of the carts: they had panels, and ... on the panels that were between the frames were lions, oxen, and cherubim.... On the plates of its flanges ... he engraved cherubim, lions, and palm trees...*
>
> *(1 Kings 7: 13-36)*

> *Then the priests brought in the ark of the covenant of the Lord to its place into the inner sanctuary of the temple, to the Most Holy Place, under the wings of the cherubim. For the cherubim spread their two wings over the place of the ark, and the cherubim overshadowed the ark and its poles.*
>
> *(I Kings 8:6-7)*

Anointing oil is used during Orthodox services to sanctify those who are anointed. It is a symbol of the Holy Spirit and was used extensively in ancient Temple worship.

> *Then Moses took the anointing oil and anointed the tabernacle and all that was in it, and sanctified them. He sprinkled some of it on the altar seven times, anointed the altar and all its utensils, and the laver and its base, to sanctify them. And he poured some of the anointing oil on Aaron's head and anointed him, to sanctify him....*
>
> *(Leviticus 8:10-12)*

by Fr. A. James Bernstein

In an Orthodox Christian service, a cantor-deacon leads the people in worship as he chants petitions to God. The practice of chanting prayers is inherited from both Temple and synagogue worship. At two points in the service processions are made, similar to those made to the ancient Temple and the carrying of the Torah within the synagogue. Periodically during the service, the priest faces the people and, as they stand, blesses them as the kings of Israel and the priests did in ancient Israel. "And the king turned around and blessed the whole congregation of Israel, while all the congregation of Israel was standing. (*I Kings 8:14*)

> *Then the priests, the Levites, arose and blessed the people, and their voice was heard; and their prayer came up to His holy dwelling place, to heaven.* (*II Chronicles 30:27*)

As the Jews show their deepest respects by kissing and venerating the Torah and *mezuzahs*, the Orthodox Christian kisses and venerates the Holy Gospels, the crosses, and icons. In doing so, neither are worshipping that which they venerate. Rather both are expressing their love by venerating that which they deeply respect.

The high point of the Orthodox service is the re-presenting of the sacrifice of Christ to God the Father and partaking of this sacrifice at communion. During the *anaphora*, elevation, and fraction, the priest represents on behalf of the people, the once-for-all sacrifice of Christ. He does not re-sacrifice Christ but re-presents His sacrifice. This is done as the ancient priests sacrificed the Passover lamb on behalf of the people.

> *So the service was prepared, and the priests stood in their places, and the Levites in their divisions, according to the king's command. And they slaughtered the Passover offerings; and the priests sprinkled the blood with their hands while the Levites skinned the animals...Also they roasted the Passover offerings with fire ... and divided them quickly among all the lay people.* (*II Chronicles 35:10-13*)

In the ancient Temple, the people ate of the offerings after they were sacrificed. So likewise Orthodox Christians partake of the re-presented sacrifice of Christ as they eat His body and blood during communion.

I was convinced that as an evangelical Protestant, I had missed out on heavenly worship. I had missed out on that form of worship reflecting on earth, the form of worship existing in heaven. The Orthodox Christian Divine Liturgy, I became convinced, reflects heavenly worship and thereby also retains the essence of ancient Temple worship, now fulfilled in the Messiah. Its authenticity enabled me to worship fully, both spiritually and physically, in the tradition of early Jewish-Christian worship. With icons and incense, with multi-colored vestments and ringing bells, with flickering candle light, melodious chant and processions, with cycles of feast days and fasts, Judaism is fulfilled in Christ and our praise ascends to God. We on earth mystically join with those in heaven, together lifting up holy hands towards Him who sits upon the celestial throne. Together we sing, "Holy, Holy, Holy, Lord God Almighty, heaven and earth are filled with your glory!"

Discovering Christian Roots

Deeply impressed with Orthodox Christian worship, I began to consider seriously the continuity of the historical Orthodox Church. As a Jew, having roots had always been important to me. I now contemplated the importance of having Christian roots as well.

I often meet evangelical Christians who tell me, "I am Jewish, too!" Most often, they are gentile Christians who not only think of themselves as being "spiritually" Jewish, but have also convinced themselves that they are physically Jews. Though it is flattering that they would want to consider themselves as such (Where were all these people during W.W.II?), I cannot help but think that they are deluding themselves. To be a Jew, it seem to me, is to be physically and historically part of the Jewish people. It's to be part of a people in flesh, in history, in birth, and death -- not only in sympathy or respect. The rest, as Saint Paul writes, must be grafted in.

Many evangelical Protestants and Jewish-Christians are the same when it comes to religion. Both groups share a tendency to "spiritualize" everything, often at the cost of the physical. As a Jew, I was beginning to realize that the Church is every bit as physical and historical as the Jewish people. As an authentic Jew who is proud of his heritage, I was beginning to desire to be an authentic Christian in an authentic Christian Church. I knew my evangelical Protestant brethren to be authentic Christians who "knew" Jesus, were living holy lives, and were heaven bound. But did

by Fr. A. James Bernstein

this mean they automatically manifested the Church? I was not sure. I was sure of one thing: I didn't want to be in a make-believe Church. Rather, I wanted to be in that Church which is historically connected with the ancient Jewish-Christian Church.

Certainly, the Orthodox Church has clearly identifiable roots. She has a historical continuity of doctrine which can be traced back to the Apostles. This deposit of truth, called Holy Tradition, was passed down faithfully from person to person, and from generation to generation. Orthodox lineage was certainly visible, discernible, and historical. The Church claims to be, as the Apostle Paul said, the "pillar and ground of the truth" (*I Timothy 3:15*).

In addition to this succession of truth, there is another succession the Orthodox Church honors -- succession of bishops, the apostolic continuity which is rooted in the ancient Jewish-Christian Church. The New Testament reveals that from the very beginning the Apostles established individuals within local Churches who functioned as apostolic representatives and were called bishops (*episcopoi* in Greek).

Numerous, readily available early accounts reveal that the office of bishops existed universally in the early Church. Bishops were present everywhere while the Church was still illegal and being persecuted by the Roman Empire. They were not a later "corruption," but present in the Church from the beginning. For instance, the great martyr and bishop of Antioch, Ignatius, lived in the first century! He wrote: "Let all men respect the deacons as they reverence Jesus Christ, just as they must respect the bishops as the counterpart of the Father, and the presbyters as the council of God, and the college of the apostles; without these no Church is recognized" (*St. Ignatius to the Trallians, 3*).

Irenaeus of Lyons, at the end of the second Century, likewise wrote: "Those who wish to see the truth can observe in every Church the tradition of the Apostles made manifest in the whole world. We can enumerate those who were appointed bishops in the Churches by the Apostles, and their successors, down to our own day" (*Irenaeus' Against Heresies, III, 3*).

Though I realized that the succession of bishops does not automatically assure a succession of truth, apostolic continuity did seem to be God's intent for His Church. As a Jew, it made good sense to me, for it helped provide a physical and tangible link as well as a spiritual link with the ancient Jewish-Christian Church.

The Church of the Holy Land

Back in June of 1967, I happened to be living just outside Jerusalem when the Six Day War broke out. Following the war I was among the first to move into the old city of Jerusalem from the new city. I lived with Arab Christians only a few blocks from where my father was born. During my year's stay there I had many opportunities to visit the holy sites and churches in Jerusalem. The Protestant side of me had difficulty appreciating the more ornate and traditional Churches. But as I met Jerusalem Christians, I came to realize that the indigenous Arab Christians in the Holy Land are neither Protestant nor Roman Catholic. They are Orthodox! The Bible in *Acts 1:8* says that prior to His ascension, the Lord Jesus told the Apostles, "You shall receive power when the Holy Spirit has come upon you; and you shall be witnesses to Me in Jerusalem, and in all Judea and Samaria, and to the end of the earth."

The Orthodox Church is the indigenous Church in the Middle East and in the Holy Land, the land of the Bible and of our ancient Jewish forefathers. The Orthodox Church existed for a millennium and a half before Protestantism was born. From this Jerusalem birthplace, Orthodox Christianity spread west to Rome and Greece, north to Europe and Russia, south to Egypt, and east to Persia and India. As I recalled my Holy Land experience, I cannot help but think there is a providential purpose in the continuous presence of Orthodox Christianity in the Holy Land -- just as there is for the continued existence of the Jewish people.

The Orthodox Church is more than a mystical body of believers. She is also an institutional, concrete, and historical reality with clearly recognizable expansion. As the indigenous Church in the Holy Land, the Orthodox Church can be traced back to the beginning -- to Christ Himself and to the Apostles. This physical, historical continuity rooted in the Holy Land is very meaningful to me as a Jewish-Christian.

Rediscovering the God of the Jews

I was impressed with Orthodox Christian worship, roots, and origin. Her worship I found to be divine, her roots deep, and her origin in the Holy Land. As a Jewish-Christian, I was strongly drawn to Orthodoxy. But what about Orthodox theology? How did the Orthodox view of God compare with the Protestant view? How did it relate to the Jewish view?

by Fr. A. James Bernstein

As a child, I had often prayed, "Hear, O Israel: The Lord our God, the Lord is one," (*Deuteronomy 6:4*). Later as a Protestant Christian, I longed for the Judaic emphasis of worshipping God as Creator and King. Though I believed in the Trinity and in the Divinity of Christ and of the Holy Spirit, I was often confused over questions such as how the Son and the Holy Spirit related to the Father or to whom I should direct my prayers. I discovered that Orthodox Christians primarily direct their worship to God the Father. The Orthodox believe there is One God because there is One Father.

I knew that the word "God" in the New Testament almost always refers to God the Father. I also knew that the Son and the Holy Spirit are often spoken of as being of God as in "Son of God" or the "Spirit of God." But why didn't the Bible say "Father of God?" The reason, the Orthodox explained, is that the Father is not of God but is God. This emphasis on God the Father as the source of unity within the Trinity was lacking in my Protestant experience. Yet it seemed to me to be very Jewish, for it explained more clearly the relationship of God the Son and God the Holy Spirit to God the Father.

Orthodoxy, I discovered, teaches clearly that both the Son and the Holy Spirit have their eternal origin in the Father, fully sharing the complete divine nature with Him. The Father is called the fountain head of the Trinity, the eternal source of the Godhead, and His headship is the unity of the Three Persons. So that is why Orthodoxy speaks of the Father first, and it explains why the Apostle Paul often greets the Church to whom he is writing by saying: "I thank my God through Jesus Christ for you all..." (*Romans 1:8*) or, "Grace to you and peace from God our Father and the Lord Jesus Christ" (*Ephesians 1:2*).

This is also why the Nicene Creed says: "I believe in one God, the Father Almighty, Creator of heaven and earth, and of all things visible and invisible; and in one Lord Jesus Christ, the Son of God.... And I believe in the Holy Spirit, the Lord, and Giver of Life, Who proceeds from the Father...."

In worshipping God the Father as Creator of the universe, as the King of Israel, and as God and Father of Our Lord Jesus Christ, I was now beginning to learn how to worship God as my New Testament Jewish-Christian brethren did.

Rediscovering Our True Sacrifice

In 1967 I visited the Wailing Wall and walked about the Temple mount where the ancient Jewish Temple once stood. I was struck with the centrality of Temple worship and sacrifice for the ancient Jews. The Old Testament clearly shows that the sacrificial system was an integral part of the Jewish religion and of Temple worship. I knew from reading Jewish history that with the destruction of the Jewish Temple and the cessation of the sacrificial system in the first century, devout Jews were thrown into great confusion. Many of the Jewish people were sympathetic to the Pharisees who decided sacrifice was not necessary. They held that prayers and good deeds could replace sacrifice. So, they emphasized synagogue worship rather than Temple worship. Such is the inheritance of present day Judaism.

On the other hand, many devout Jews became Christians and held that Christ, the Lamb of God, has been provided by God the Father as the fulfillment of the Temple's sacrificial system. The early Jewish-Christians saw Christ as a new and superior sacrifice, of which the earthly Temple sacrifices were only types. At Communion we re-present Christ's once-for-all Sacrifice to God the Father.

I knew from reading the New Testament that Communion was not an optional act of worship. The book of Acts says the disciples continued "daily with one accord in the temple, and breaking bread from house to house...." Yet, as an evangelical Protestant, Communion had become optional for me. It had been relegated to second class status behind preaching and even in some cases, music. The infrequency of Communion in many churches proved how very far worship had moved from the Biblical and Jewish Church model. I knew I was missing the full form and glory of Communion worship and I desperately wanted to regain it. In the Orthodox worship service, I felt God's presence. I was entering into fulfilled Temple worship, through Christ's authentic sacrifice.

Rediscovering Jewish Mysticism

In the Orthodox Church I was also beginning to rediscover holy mystery. I love mystery, I suppose, because God Himself is not only awesome, He is mysterious. Jews are considered to be mysterious people. Modern rationalists disdain mystery, but Orthodox Christians thrive on it. In fact, Saint Paul calls our very life in Christ a "mystery."

by Fr. A. James Bernstein

The English word "mystery" comes from the Greek term *mysterion* which means anything hidden or secret. The biblical Greek concept, though, does not mean a secret for which no answer can be found. Rather, it is a temporary secret, which is being revealed by God to men through His Spirit. The concept of mystery is close to a Greek word *apokalypsis* which is translated into the English as "revelation."

As a Jew, then, I discovered worship that contained a sense of mystery, rooted in ancient Jewish practice, and centered upon God and our Communion meal with Him. But the worship I experienced as an evangelical Protestant tended to view mystical worship as dangerous because it went beyond "reason." This was particularly true of the Communion service.

I had been taught as a new Christian that the bread and wine of Communion were symbols and nothing more. To go beyond this was to risk falling into a "magical" view of Communion. Though I had read in the Bible that our Lord Jesus said of the Communion bread, "This is my body" and of the cup of wine, "This is my blood," I was told that the bread and wine merely "signified" body and blood.

This rationalistic view of Communion appealed to my mind, but not to my heart. I wondered, is there something missing? After all, had not Saint Paul said in *First Corinthians 11:29-30*, "For he who eats and drinks in an unworthy manner eats and drinks judgment to himself, not discerning the Lord's body. For this reason many are weak and sick among you, and many sleep." Why were those who partook in an ungodly way becoming sick and dying if the bread and wine were nothing more than symbols?

In discussing this matter with my Orthodox Christian friends, I discovered a number of things I had not known. For example, the records from the first three centuries tell us that the Church universally held the Eucharistic bread and wine to be the Body and Blood of Christ! The ancient Church did not attempt to explain how. Instead, they simply referred to Communion as "O Great Mystery!" I also discovered that the concept of the Eucharist as a symbol and nothing more did not really arise until the radical Protestant Reformation -- a millennium and a half after the founding of the Church!

No wonder that the evangelical Protestant Churches I attended always seemed so "bare bones" and void of mystery. They were empty not because God and faith were absent; in fact, many Protestant Christians were very vibrant and alive. But in pursuing a rationalistic approach to spiritual truth Protestant worship had unwittingly lost God's mystery.

For the most part, the early Protestant reformers had reacted against what they saw as a magical understanding of the Eucharist implicit in medieval Roman practice. Furthermore -- and here most Orthodox would agree -- the reformers were impatient with the scholastic form of Rome's teaching of the Eucharist that tended to formalize mystery.

The Orthodox Church presented me with a New Testament balance. On the one hand, the Orthodox Church does not seek to explain mystery as does the Roman Church; and on the other hand, it does not deny mystery as many Protestant Churches do. Mystery in the Eucharist is preserved, permeating the Faith and providing at every Communion service the reality of God's presence in our midst.

Orthodoxy reawakened in me a sense of the awe of God and life, a sense of wonder and of mystery. I was reminded of the great acts of God in history: the creation of the world, the Flood, the delivery of the Hebrews from Egyptian bondage, the birth and life of Christ, our Lord's Resurrection, the healing ministry of the Apostles. As a Jew, I longed to experience God as supernatural mystery. In light of all that God has done, it was not difficult for me to believe that, if God so chose, He could make bread and wine to be also, in a mystery, the Body and Blood of Christ.

Rediscovering the Joy of the Lord

Jews love to celebrate! Maybe it's because we have suffered so much. We take every opportunity we can to give thanks, even if the event seems to be small.

As a new Christian, I missed the intensity of Jewish asceticism (praying and fasting) and also the intensity of Jewish mirth. I missed the happy music, the folk dancing, the magnificent combining of feasting and asceticism that is uniquely Jewish. It is a paradox that in order to truly and fully celebrate one must also know how to truly and fully sacrifice, pray, and fast. It is therefore no coincidence that an Orthodox Jew would know how to do both, because the two streams of spirituality -- the ascetic and the festal -- encourage and enhance one another.

Without celebration I found myself drowning in a sea of starkness. There was no tradition of dance. Many forbade wine and discouraged any type of celebrating that might demonstrate too much festivity. Joyous celebration often was seen as being "of the world." Mystical celebrating was foreign. Since it was a major problem to know how we Christians would celebrate, we often did little or nothing, to be on the safe side.

I found the Orthodox Church to be sensitive to the centrality of celebration as a fundamental and obvious human need. As an Orthodox Christian, one knows how to and what to celebrate. Celebrating festal holidays is part of the Orthodox Christian tradition rooted in the Bible.

When Orthodox Christians celebrate Easter (*Pascha*), for example, they don't just celebrate one day: they celebrate for almost two weeks! Both before Easter and Christmas, moreover, there are many days during which they prepare for the celebrations through intense prayer and fasting.

The proper joining of the sacrificial and festal streams of spirituality is a work of God. Orthodox Christians know how to celebrate, for the Church has lived two millennia under the guidance of the Holy Spirit. As a struggling Christian who finds it difficult to develop any degree of spirituality, I find it a wonderful relief to know that my life struggles can be punctuated at many glorious times along the way with feasting.

As the Church's human face is revealed to us, her heavenly face is not forgotten. Our Lord Jesus said: "Therefore you shall be perfect, just as your Father in heaven is perfect" (*Matthew 5:48*). The Orthodox Faith presents the highest possible goal for us to pursue, the ideal of perfection: to become by grace what God is by nature. Ideal standards and saintly lives are set forward in Scripture and in the Church to inspire us in our struggle. These ideals include the concepts of poverty, chastity, fidelity, obedience -- fleshed out in practice by those who give all to the poor (*Matthew 19:21*), love their enemies (*Matthew 5:43-48*), submit to spiritual authority (*Matthew 8:5-13; John 5:19*), pray constantly (*Ephesians 6:18; I Thessalonians 5:17*), and live holy and blameless lives.

On the other hand, I found that the Orthodox Church recognizes that we are far from what we should be. With this in mind, She accepts us as sinners, while continuing to condemn our sins. She does not lower the standard to which we are called but offers forgiveness and healing to our human weaknesses and sins. Recognizing our human frailty, the Church is concerned not to overwhelm us spiritually, but to accept us where we are and lead us step by step towards God. This sensitivity to human frailty, this human face of Orthodoxy, I found to be very Jewish.

Coming Home

As a Jewish-Christian, I became convinced I would be at home in the Orthodox Church. The Church provides worship of God that is Biblically based. She has a sacrifice on earth reflecting that which is offered in heaven. She has clear continuity of history going back to Christ and the Apostles, and is the original Church of the Holy Land. Orthodox Christianity respects divine mystery and does not press for false clarity. And she provides both an ascetic and festive ideal, being at the same time sensitive to our human frailty. Most of all, I found the Orthodox Church was in continuity with the ancient Jewish-Christian Church.

On Christmas Eve, 1981, I was received into the Orthodox Christian Church. My wife, Bonnie, and our four children -- Heather, Holly, Peter, and Mary -- also became Orthodox. Subsequently, I've been to seminary and have been ordained an Orthodox priest.

I extend to my Jewish-Christian brethren an earnest invitation. Come, visit the Orthodox Church. Spend a month of Sundays with us. Experience the worship, the mystery, the majesty, the centrality of the Messiah which springs from the pages of the New Testament and is rooted in the Old. Discover the Jewish-Christian Church that our Lord Jesus established, into which people from every nation, tongue, and tribe have come, and become truly Orthodox.

When Words Take Flesh

by William Barlow

I grew up in an evangelical environment where being Christian meant having had a conversion experience in which Christ had been received into a person's life as his Savior. That was the test and the reason people went to church. Worship was simple and therefore thought to be superior, consisting of hymns, prayers, and a sermon, all celebrating each person's certainty of having been saved. Consequently, it was very sincere. Even so, such worship was descriptive of a state of alienation, deliberately cultivated, where those participating stood apart from other people because they had not received Christ into their lives, and from the world because it had played no positive part in bringing them either to Christ or to a knowledge of God.

At Sunday School, however, we were not expected to have had a conversion experience, being too young. Instead, we were invited to befriend a Jesus who had said that little children could always come to Him, and who was so immediately accessible as to make it seem the most natural thing in the world to do so. So natural, in fact, that religion did not enter into it.

I was glad because religious people made me feel uncomfortable. Such was the impact of the Gospel stories upon me, however, that I quickly sensed that being Christian meant being human. My idea of a personal relationship with Christ, therefore, became centered on the image I had of Him, derived from the Gospels, and it was such a human one that I instinctively looked for it in others, it seeming only natural to do so. Being Christian was not something I saw as setting me apart because I was saved and others were not. On the contrary, I believed that insofar as mine was a truly human life, it was inseparable from others, whether Christian or not.

Although worship was Christ-centered, because it was about being saved by him, it did not seem to put Christ at the center of life where I instinctively knew He should be. Also, the world appeared not to be included in worship and this especially made me feel uncomfortable in church. Worship failed to do justice to all I believed. Consequently, my relationship with Christ seemed not to suffer by my not going to church.

This disparity between belief and worship resulting from the priority given to faith derived from a particular kind of conversion experience applied not only to evangelical practice. All worship seemed seriously flawed by its having an auxiliary role. For me, belief and worship had to be one, in church as well as out of it. That has been the key to my religious development and the reason I became Orthodox.

So, without realizing what was happening to me because it did not involve being religious, I learned to worship in spite of the church. Rather, my capacity for worship showed itself whenever I did something which totally absorbed me. No one ever told me, of course, that this had anything to do with worship. Since worship for them meant hymns and prayers with a sermon, all they saw was a child at play.

This blinded them, as it does others, to the possible implications of being totally involved in something. In my case these implications were far-reaching because what absorbed me very early on was playing with toy soldiers. At first I used them to stage battles, but then I began to take enormous pleasure in parading them. I spent hours doing this without being bored because what absorbed me, increasingly, was the imagery involved. I found the sight of toy soldiers immaculately arrayed intensely satisfying and derived a contemplative delight at perceiving stillness in models of marching men, and movement in those adopting a static pose. Soon I had an image of the perfect toy soldier which I learned could be conveyed even where a model was damaged. Somehow, that seemed not to matter. On the other hand, there were models which, although intact, did not measure up to the image of the perfect toy soldier.

My interest in imagery did not end there. Behind the image of the toy soldier lay another: that of real soldiers, and my mind was always switching from one to the other. From appreciating a well-made toy soldier I moved easily to admiration of the real thing and, it being wartime, there were always plenty of them around.

I very early began also to take an interest in the badges which soldiers wore on their caps and started to collect them. These, too, were images, and they impressed me because they were always symbolic of a living tradition of service and sacrifice. Whenever I handled a badge I was aware of the history behind it, and that it had been worn by someone.

Irrespective of what was depicted, the image conveyed to me was that of the perfect soldier and because I admired soldiers for their human qualities of courage and selflessness, that also of the ideal man. Thus it was that a profoundly Christian attitude to man, based on imagery, took root in my life.

Now if you ask a child what he wants to do when he grows up, he may say he wants to be a train driver. Here, being and doing are one. Acquiring an image may therefore occasion growth to a point where what one does no longer suffices for what one has become. This can happen in the army where the image of soldier continually draws upon that of man. The implications are far-reaching.

Meanwhile school encouraged the pursuit of images. There we learnt to think vocationally, which didn't mean being called by God necessarily, but simply serving others. There were recognized ways of doing this, all involving imagery. The army was one of them, being regarded as much a vocation as that of doctor, teacher, or priest. These also involved meaningful careers conferring status and a place in society. Nevertheless, selflessness took priority, enhancing the image enormously. Where this entailed centering one's self on something to the exclusion of all else, it was not only a sense of vocation which was being encouraged but also our instinct for worship.

I now began to cultivate the image of the perfect soldier, taking advantage of the provision enabling boys to enlist at 16 to be groomed for leadership. I saw no contradiction in being both a soldier and a Christian. I understood being Christian to mean responding to God: some used the Bible as their sole guide, others used the Bible drawing on the Church's experience. But Christ sometimes said things which so eclipse any notion of a calculated, officially approved response as to carry authority even with unbelievers. No one loves more, He declared, than he who lays down his life for others. This was enough for me. I saw this as the principle from which all service to others derives and none can embrace it without entering the divine realm. This makes soldiering a challenging and paradoxical experience incurring great risk: not that of losing one's life but finding it.

Soon after enlisting, I saw a Guards drill display. In *Goodbye to All That*, Robert Graves observes that drill "as it should be done is beautiful, especially when it feels itself as a whole and each movement is not a synchronized movement of every man together, but the single movement of a large creature." This goes beyond precision to a point where being and doing are one, as happens in oriental martial artistry which is always regarded as a spiritual way. Indeed, Antoine St. Exupery has said that "spiritual life begins when a human being is seen to be more than the sum of his component parts." Watching this squad drill as though it had access to some fundamental law of life, I felt nevertheless confronted by a most articulate statement of regimental identity that owed itself to a capacity for human oneness which their training had drawn out. I felt involved in what they were as human beings but excluded from what they were as soldiers and, as a soldier myself, I was amazed. If that is what training can do, I thought, I must join them. So I did, by transferring into the Irish Guards. Thus were my career plans overturned. Having joined the army as a form of Christian service, I was now to discover it as a spiritual way.

The army is essentially a life. You cannot be a soldier without entering into the life of your regiment. In Bugles and a Tiger, John Masters says that the "continentality" one feels as a soldier relates to the life one lives with one's comrades rather than the loss felt when a comrade is killed. John Donne, he recalls, spoke of continentality in terms of "every man's death decreases me because I am involved in Mankinde." Masters, however, and with genius, draws out what he calls "the other half of Donne's parable --- any man's life *increases* me because I am involved in Mankinde." This is the more immediate truth a soldier has to deal with and as Masters says, "it goes even closer to the center" of regimental continentality.

For Peter Davies, a Gurkha officer, being a soldier meant "sharing an intensity of living ... that I had not experienced before nor have since." Nothing, he relates, "had stretched me so far." It is true that the demands made upon soldiers call upon a great deal of life within them. Yet these demands are not physical merely. They cannot be met without a spirited response involving courage, selflessness, team spirit, and high endeavor. This explains perhaps, the writer R. W. Thompson's love for the army. It taught him, he says, "to live more fully."

This fullness certainly owed much to the relatedness between men which training results in and which takes no heed of race, color or creed. None of the churches can claim this, for while they may indeed embrace people of different races and color, they cannot by definition include either atheists or those not of their own creed. A regiment can. "When we unfurl our colors," proclaimed an Indian Army officer, "we put our religion in our knapsacks." No soldier who has experienced this can ever again look upon organized religion with the same eyes.

As for the intensity of life, it enhances self-awareness, making one feel more human. One grows precisely because one has been involved in mankind to an extent which can be very difficult to assimilate. Masters, in *The Road Past Mandalay*, says as much when he speaks of "the expansion of my capacity as a human being." Nevertheless he makes sense, to me at least, when he says that "the growth was ... due ... to the humanness of others touching me.... In an odd and special way I felt I had physically absorbed something of all men and all women."

When this happens, the body no longer serves merely to distinguish one man from another. It becomes a criterion for a different kind of integrity where the final truth each man lives is that we are all one flesh.

This experience, born in hardship, was an ascetic one since the body's potential for life was revealed in its very limitations. One saw the body as the only proper means of expressing all the life one is capable of. Yet one recognized also its inability to do so in its present state. Consequently, I felt a burning desire to die so as to be given a new body, such as could fully express this plenitude of life. This was the first experience I had which pointed towards a resurrection of the body as both a possibility and a need for the newly discovered life to make sense.

This asceticism also impinged upon the army's obsession with the image of the perfect soldier which can only be realized in the life each man draws out of himself. This image is, therefore, constantly being put to a test: that of life. It raises the question, in an acute form, of whether the image of the perfect soldier does justice to that of man. The Christian implications of this are far-reaching.

A surprising discovery was that soldiering is a life of non-resistance. Obeying orders is about setting self aside and giving in, and the more one obeys, the more passive one becomes. "Those who are put over us," declared Admiral Anson, "if they act the part, we ought to reverence. If they do not, I say no. None of your passive obedience and non-resistance." Strict discipline makes it possible to practice non-resistance unceasingly. There was always a human dimension, an unfair order, perhaps, or a bullying NCO. So the opportunity was always there to turn the other cheek. In such situations those in authority believed they were doing something to a man. He, however, could transform the situation by, as it were, allowing them to do it. Thus, occasions of discipline could be used to obey Christ's words, to affirm life, and to assert one's solidarity even with those at whose hands one suffered. Non-resistance, therefore, entered into the very fabric of one's life, making one a good soldier and adding profoundly to one's sense of continentality. Non-resistance could also be practiced in the total absence of war and I became committed to it without becoming a pacifist. The Gospel, I learned, is bigger than pacifism.

Meanwhile, I became fascinated by the use made of the voice, for if the aim of drill was to make men one, it was through the voice that this was done. As an instructor, I learned that one could pour all that one is into what one said, making every word count. Not only one's commitment to the army, but also one's belief in man invested everything one said with an evangelical intent, inviting others to share one's vision of life. Such earnest endeavor, centered on words, involving as it did the body, resulted in an extraordinary inner unity which found its focus, not in the mind, but in the heart.

Thus it was that by shouting unceasingly, and always in pursuit of exalted ends, the somatopsychic mechanism associated with prayer of the heart was activated. A great purity entered into everything one did, enabling one to see in a way that had a burning quality. Yet one's sobriety increased and a deep stillness held sovereignty within. One now saw the training of men with different eyes and with even greater fascination. When squads drilled well it was because they assimilated perfectly what had been said to them. Then they moved naturally with a relaxed style suggestive of a primeval innocence. Words, in fact, seemed, literally, to have taken flesh.

This might have been the peak of my army experience but for something that happened as I was getting into bed at the end of a typical day of drilling men. I was about to lie down when I became aware that someone was standing in the corner of the room. It was dark and I could see no one, but the sense that someone was definitely there was very strong. Naturally, I wondered who it could be, but even as I asked the question, whoever it was moved across the room towards me, still unseen, until there was no longer any distance between us. To put it crudely, it was as though he had stepped into me rather like a ghost steps into a wall in a movie. Immediately this happened, I became aware of changes taking place in my body. A warm tingling sensation began to spread with enlivening effect, causing the fulcrum of self-awareness to shift from the mind into the body, giving it an acute alertness and intelligence. I seemed to come alive in a completely new way, the body becoming a focus for moral worth and spiritual vitality so tremendous that it seemed to have been translated into another realm, that of love.

I still did not know who this person was and, as though to get an answer, I extended my arms in front of me to look at him, for everything was centered on the body. As I asked myself what was the life pulsating throughout my entire being, the words of Christ, of the Beatitudes, immediately came to mind. There was a perfect correspondence between them and what was happening to my body. They had, it seemed, taken flesh in me. Thus it was that I knew who this person was who had come to me in that room and that Christ was risen indeed.

✠ ✠ ✠ ✠ ✠ ✠

I now took steps to train to become an army chaplain.

By the time I was at theological college certain ideas had seized the imagination of Christians who believed the churches were out of touch with society. John Robinson's *Honest To God*, in particular, had an enormous impact and there was much talk of the need for religion to be relevant to life. Because "mankind had come of age" Christianity should be religionless, which entailed "secularizing the Gospel." But in that case what do you do about worship, and where does the world fit into it?

These questions preoccupied us and I was fascinated to see how inept the churches were in coping with them. Worship, surely, is the one thing they should know about. Why then, I wondered, couldn't they answer even their own questions about it?

I felt very involved, for while the problems were being treated as though they were new, I thought otherwise. Religion had always meant more to me out-of-doors and I had learned to believe in spite of worship. With hindsight I now see my enlistment as directly related to this predicament. Certainly I was attracted to the military, but at a deeper level my becoming a soldier was an attempt to establish the place of worship in my life.

My endeavors to understand our problems therefore became very personal and centered on my army experience. There were two reasons for this.

The first was that the army had enabled me to practice what was in effect a form of religionless Christianity. But whereas my colleagues were stumbling about not knowing quite what the expression meant, yet advocating the demolition of churches, I had a good idea of what I meant and I was not convinced that church buildings were redundant.

This is worth noting, given that soldiering so filled my life that formal worship was entirely peripheral to it. I felt absolutely no need to go to church. In the field we needed a simple faith, the simpler the better. This I had, and the army enabled me to turn everything I did into an expression of commitment and belief. There was no correspondence at all between what we did in the field and in church that I could see. I thought there should be. An Eastern ascetic has said that piety means being in touch with yourself. We were, and it put us at variance with many of those who went to church. We owed this to the regiment in which we lived, moved, and had our being. The regiment was a far greater reality to us and was the only real society of which we had any experience. Yet instinct told me that the answer was not to do away with churches. What I expected was that worship should correspond to the depths which our intensely purposeful lives had revealed within us. For the regiment was also a vehicle of growth and personal emergence and there was nothing vague about this. Our training formed us, as it was meant to, according to an image of man which was both pursued and realized within ourselves but in relation to each other.

The second reason the army became crucial to my thinking about worship was that it had been my "world." So much theological discussion about bringing the world into worship was weakened by the failure to identify what "world" should mean in this context. All too often our debate presumed upon a common experience which applied only at the most superficial level and this showed in what was done to make worship "relevant." Nearly always, worship was devalued and became even banal. Many realized this but remained at a loss as to what to do about it.

For me, on the other hand, the army as my "world" was actually identifiable, a community set apart, living by its own laws and hugely motivated. It became meaningful to me, however, as an arena of ascetic endeavor, something I had never expected. This was because the pursuit of a specific image, deemed worthy of the perfect soldier, required the stripping away of all false images. The process was very testing indeed, precisely because it involved the inner man. One was continually having to overcome oneself because obedience entails setting self aside. Yet one engaged the army also, which is to say the "world," and had to overcome it if one was to be one's self. In so doing, one was confronted, I am sure, by what St. Paul refers to as a principality, dominion and power, for the point to grasp is that the army is impressive precisely because it incarnates, as it were, and magnificently too, the spirit of this world. Because it does so, because the world is indeed good, one can lose one's soul to it. Yet one can discover one's soul, too, but in order to keep it, one must overcome this wonderfully seductive world. Therein lies the paradox and also the key to understanding the place of the world in worship, for it has one.

My expectations of worship, therefore, were much more demanding than those of my colleagues who, essentially, were looking for cosmetic changes. Their concern was with doing; mine was with being. The realization of an image of man through ascetic endeavor located in "the world" had affected me deeply. It had awakened in me a profound awareness that the world has a sacramental significance which can be summed up in man. I expected worship to correspond to the experience which had made that insight possible. I was hoping that it would help me to cope with something more mysterious still, which was that the sacramental significance of the world somehow resided in me also because I was, myself, a man. It did neither of these things. The experience therefore remained imprisoned within, leaving me in a predicament which could not be resolved by rational analysis. For the truths involved were not such as could be thought through. They could only be lived through. Thus was the scene set for my meeting with the Eastern Church.

✠   ✠   ✠   ✠   ✠   ✠

My encounter with Orthodoxy followed the classic path of meeting with a significant spiritual figure followed by attendance at a Liturgy in an Orthodox monastery.

I first saw Metropolitan Anthony some years before on a TV discussion with some soldiers about the nature of courage. He immediately impressed me. I next saw him during theological training, having read his book *Living Prayer*, which I then put to the test. It worked and God, putting a question, spoke to me in prayer. When I told the Metropolitan he sent me to a monastery. So I went there quite literally to get the answer to a prayer.

At first, on arrival, there was the sudden appalling realization of what I had done in going to the monastery. I could not go back to what I had left behind me. Either the prayer would have to be answered or my entire spiritual life would be annulled. I felt very alone and the friendliness of the monks did nothing to dispel this.

My first impression of the monastic church was of warmth and familiarity, as though the experience I had brought with me, my experience of soldiering and of "the world," was somehow present in the liturgical action of the priest and two monks. I felt at home in a way I believed should be possible in church but which, until then, never had been. I do not believe this was a question of aesthetics, of saying, as many would, that I had at last found something that suited my own personal taste. Man's spiritual home is the Kingdom and its claim upon him is absolute because that is where he belongs and for which he is destined. Certainly I felt the claim being made upon me was total and too human to be regarded in relative terms. Moreover, in circumstances having all the paraphernalia of religion, to an extent not found anywhere else, I perceived that I was in an essentially religionless situation where I was able to be myself. I felt totally involved in the mystery before me. I knew I could never again bring to the world the same degree of involvement as before. Yet I saw, too, that it was precisely the degree of involvement in the world and amongst men that the Army had made possible which was making me receptive to this situation.

Then there was the strong sense that the liturgical action constituted a body of belief whose wholeness and integrity was such that it could be infringed upon only at the cost of standing outside what it was and represented. I realized I was inside and immediately recognized that denominational differences *are* significant and real, not something to be treated lightly as having no spiritual ramification.

As a corollary of what I have just said, however, it seemed essential to me that if one could speak of Orthodoxy in an exclusive sense, it had to be in the interest of the greatest truth possible as against a smaller one, not only as a witness to the true and living God, but also for the sake of man. The appeal then, for me, was not simply that this liturgical situation was more comprehensive than any other I had known but bigger, and most importantly, bigger than the world as I had known it. This may sound presumptuous, nevertheless I am prepared to stand by the perspective in life which my military experience has given me. Writing in *Disenchantment* about his experiences in the Great War, C. E. Montague had said:

> *"Rightly or wrongly, no men who have been close friends for a year and who know that in the next few hours they are as likely as not to be killed together in doing what they hold to be right will entertain on any terms the idea of any closing of gates of divine mercy open to themselves in the face of any comrade in the business."*

Fortunately, as I saw it, this worship did not require that I should. I had served in an Irish regiment where religion divided us and convinced me that there, at any rate, the world was bigger than the church. I knew it should not be but had no evidence. Here, however, I saw that whilst it is given to each of us to choose for one denomination as against another if we so wish, what we cannot do, in becoming Christian, is to opt out of the human race. Whatever else this worship might mean, therefore, for me it meant standing in life, not in denominational or cultic terms, but as a human being alongside all mankind.

✠　✠　✠　✠　✠　✠

On return to London I learnt that I had been short-listed for a scholarship which would enable me to study Orthodoxy in any country I wished. I decided on Greece and chose to observe the way the Greeks worshipped.

Greece became an event in my life because I went there at exactly the right moment. It proved the ideal follow-up to my stay at the monastery a few months earlier. There are times when a man's inner and outer life are in complete harmony, the one serving to confirm the other. That was the case with me. There is something about Greece, which others have remarked upon, that puts a man face to face with what he believes. The result is that one feels remarkably free, and therefore open, so that everything that happens seems full of meaning. So while I went about my studies I knew, deep down, that they were not the only reason I was in Greece. There were things I needed to know.

One concerned my future. What was I to do with my life? The Army had been a worthy form of service and I had much to give it. But it was not to be. I had moved onto training for the priesthood, also a worthy form of service, yet that was not to be, either. What then was the answer? I had no idea, not even how to begin thinking about it. Yet I was not worried. I knew something would come.

Then one evening, as I walked along the waterfront at Thessaloniki, it seemed that the question which required answering was not what I should do on return to England, but what conditions would have to be satisfied by whatever I did. To my amazement the first to occur to me was that I should die. Did that make sense? Oddly, yes.

A great deal of sense. I am not alone in having been so intensely alive as to feel keenly the need to die. At such moments indeed the life one has access to seems already to have shifted its true center to a realm not of this world. I therefore saw that I would never again be permitted to look for, or find, the kind of meaning in the world that the army had made possible. That was in the past. There would be no career, no new vocation even. This gave me absolutely no pointers at all for the future, yet I knew it made sense. So I bided my time and waited for the answer to come.

Soon afterwards, I attended a liturgy and went up into the balcony to watch the goings on, which were always interesting. For a while I was intent upon the people but then noticed how much light there was, and life. Light and life, I thought, lingering over each word. Quite suddenly I saw that light and life were indeed what characterized the worship, but not only because of the people, the candle flames reflected in the glass covering the icons, and the chandeliers plunging downwards like exploding starshells. There was another kind of light and life present because Christ was in our midst. But if that is so, I reflected, I was no longer in the world. I was standing beyond death because I was in the Kingdom. Thus it was that the worship of the Orthodox Church seemed to meet the conditions I had drawn up concerning what I was to do with my life.

There were other moments when light was suddenly thrown upon problems one had struggled with in the Western Christian situation. On one occasion I was in an empty church on a week-day when a man came in and venerated an icon. He moved very quickly and it was only after he had gone out that I realized he had his hat on all the time he was in church. That amused me but it also made me think. In the West even unbelievers instinctively remove their hats on entering church. So why hadn't he? Was it because for him there was no change when he entered the church from outside? But that seemed absurd. Orthodox churches are bizarre compared with the outside world and it is impossible not to know that you are stepping into an entirely different situation. So what was the explanation for the man's forgetfulness? Could it be that in one sense there really was no change for that man when he entered the church from outside? In that case perhaps one could think in terms, not of relevance to life, but continuity with it. If so, the correspondence lay in something within the man and what he found around him in church. That, I decided, must be the Kingdom which is within us in the world but around us in church. So, not relevance to life, but continuity with it was the condition which worship had to satisfy and here it did so admirably.

The highlight of my stay in Greece occurred on Mount Athos. It was there that everything came together and, once again, during worship. There I attended a liturgy with only three monks present, all that was left of the community. One was a hermit.

The setting was dramatic, a monastery overlooking the sea and commanding fine views of Mount Athos: within its walls, a church which appeared to fill the entire courtyard. A storm raged outside, making it seem that the monastery was under siege, and when the semantron was vigorously struck summoning us to church it was as if Drake's Drum[6] were beating, ordering us to stand to. The hostile conditions without brought out the warm intimate atmosphere inside the church, turning it into a place of refuge and I was grateful for it. I had to assume the monks were there, because I could not see them at first. Only as my eyes grew accustomed to the darkness could I make them out. I saw only two and they were already rattling through the words of the service which quickly became monotonous. So I switched off, knowing there was a long time to go.

Suddenly I sensed the need to be alert to what was happening. A third voice, that of the hermit, intervened and now took a leading part. It was quite unlike the others, very sincere, and although unmusical, superior to them. The way in which the words were delivered carried authority and compelled attention. There was no vain repetition here and

---

6   According to the popular legend, when England is in danger, the drum of Sir Francis Drake, now lodged in the West Country, mysteriously beats. Some claim to have heard it. Sir Henry Newbolt wrote about it in a poem, "Drake's Drum" (1914).

no heartless detachment, whilst the Byzantine acoustics seemed to capture the words as though to hold them up before the Christ Pantocrator soaring above us. I automatically looked up and then down to where the hermit stood totally involved in what he was singing. A fleeting intimation of that monastic aloneness which I had seen elsewhere on the Holy Mountain crossed my mind. It had not always impressed me, but this seemed different for it was the aloneness of a deliberate choice that enables a man to get close to prayer. Here, I believed, was the true monk and his involvement in the words of prayer transformed the worship into something intimate and deeply personal. It was as though he was alone with his love and wooing the words until these were completely one with him. They seemed to take flesh so that the church became filled with their incarnate presence, so much so that it seemed the monk had become the church.

Why not, I thought, when we know that the Church is indeed a man who was Himself the Word made flesh?

I looked again at the hermit who now seemed transformed. The image of monk had fallen away and been transcended, so that it was only as *man* that justice was done to what he had achieved through prayer. Again I saw the aloneness of the true monk, yet it was the aloneness of having cast off everything that was not real. The worship came across to me as a celebration of freedom where there was nothing to detract from man fully realized, which is the true glory of God.

Getting From There to Here
by Jim Forest

My parents were people radically out-of-step with the America of the Cold War Fifties, estranged from political and religious structures that failed to challenge social patterns that create slums, unemployment, homelessness, hunger, and lynchings. In those days they both belonged to the Communist Party. I was what was sometimes called a "red-diaper baby."

Though my parents described themselves as atheists, I have come to think of them in those days as churchless believers.

An orphan raised by a Catholic farming family in western Massachusetts, my father became active in the local Catholic parish, serving as an altar boy. Inspired by a saintly pastor, he was preparing to become a priest. But the old priest was sent to another parish and his successor was a rigid man who ordered my father to resign from the local troop of Boy Scouts as it was Protestant-sponsored. His strict eyes picking out my father at Mass on Sunday, he preached against Catholic contact with those who were not in communion with Rome. My father left the church that day and never returned. Yet I gradually became aware that underneath the bitterness he had acquired toward Catholicism was grief at having lost contact with a Church which, in many ways, had shaped his conscience. Far from objecting to my own religious awakenings, he cheered me along.

My mother was also disengaged from religion. When I was eight, I recall asking her if there was a God and was impressed by the remarkable sadness in her voice when she said there wasn't. Some years later she told me she had lost her faith while a student at Smith College when a professor she admired told her that religions were only myths but were nonetheless fascinating to study. Again, as she related the story, I was struck by the sadness in her voice. Why such sadness?

My parents' love of wild life and wilderness areas had to do, I am sure, with a sense of God's nearness in places of natural beauty. For their honeymoon, they had walked a long stretch of the Appalachian Trail. Our scrap books were full of photos Dad had taken of national parks, camp sites, and forest animals. Mother used to say that Dad was a wonderful hunter, except the only thing he could aim at an animal was a camera. The idea of owning a gun was anathema to both of them.

They had a similar reverence for human beings, especially those in need or in trouble. In this regard they were more attentive to the Gospel than many who are regularly in church. Christ taught that what you do for the least person you do for him even though you may not realize it or believe in him. In this regard, my parents were high on the list of those doing what God wants us to do even if their concern for the poor had led them away from churches and into the political left. A great deal of their time went into helping people.

While I often felt embarrassed coming from a family so different from others in the neighborhood, my spiritual life was influenced by my parents' social conscience far more than I realized at the time. They made me aware that I was accountable not only for myself, my family, and friends, but for the down-and-out, the persecuted, and the unwelcome.

My parents were divorced when I was five. Afterward my mother, younger brother and I moved from Colorado to New Jersey. Our new home was in the area in which my mother had grown up, though not the same neighborhood as her wealthy parents (both were dead by the time of her return).

Mother's identification with people on the other side of the tracks had brought us to *live* on the other side of the tracks, in a small house in a mainly black neighborhood where indoor plumbing was still unusual and many local roads still unpaved. One neighbor, Libby, old as the hills and black as coal, had been born in slavery days. Earlier in her life she had worked in my grandparents' house.

Among my childhood memories is going door-to-door with my mother when she was attempting to sell subscriptions to the Communist newspaper, *The Daily Worker*. I don't recall her having any success. This experience left me with an abiding sympathy for all doorbell ringers.

We received *The Daily Worker* ourselves. It came in a plain wrapper without a return address. Occasionally Mother read aloud articles that a child might find interesting. But as the cold winds of the "McCarthy period" began to blow, the time came when, far from attempting to sell subscriptions, the fact that we were on its mailing list began to worry Mother. It was no longer thrown away with the garbage like other newspapers but was saved in drawers until autumn, then burned bit by bit with the fall leaves.

One of the nightmare experiences of my childhood was the trial and electrocution of Julius and Ethel Rosenberg, the couple accused of helping obtain US atomic secrets for the Soviet government. My parents were convinced the charges weren't true and that the Rosenbergs were scapegoats whose real crimes were being Jews and Communists. Their conviction, Mother felt, was intended to further marginalize all American Communists, along with any other groups critical of US political and economic structures, for the government wasn't only after "reds" but "pinkos." The letters the Rosenbergs sent to their children from prison were published in *The Daily Worker* and these Mother read to my brother and me. How we wept the morning after their death as she read the press accounts of their last minutes of life.

Music was part of our upbringing. Mother hadn't much of a voice, but from time to time sang with great feeling such songs as "This Land is Your Land," "Joe Hill," and "The Internationale" with its line, "Arise ye prisoners of starvation, arise ye wretched of the earth, for justice thunders condemnation, a better world's in birth." On our small wind-up 78 rpm record player, we played records of Paul Robeson, the Weavers, Burl Ives (who was a bit to the left in those days), and, of course, Pete Seeger. From these recordings I also learned many spirituals. The music of the black church was the one acceptable source of religion in the American left. I sometimes heard spirituals when I walked slowly past a nearby black church.

Despite my mother's alienation from religion, she missed the Methodist Church in which she had been raised. During the weeks surrounding Easter and Christmas, her religious homesickness got the best of her and so we attended services, sitting up in the church balcony. One year she sent my brother and me to the church's summer school. While this was a help for her as a working mother (she was a psychiatric social worker at a mental hospital), I have no doubt she hoped my brother and I would soak up the kind of information about the deeper meaning of life that she had received as a child.

The minister of the church, Rev. Roger Squire, was an exceptional man whose qualities included a gift for noticing people in balconies and connecting with children. His occasional visits to our house were delightful events. Only as an adult did it cross my mind how remarkable it was that he would make it a point to come into our neighborhood to knock on the kitchen door of a home that contained not church-goers but a Communist. One of the incidents that marked me as a child was the hospitality of the Squire family to two young women from Hiroshima and Nagasaki who had survived the nuclear bombing but were badly scarred. American religious peace groups had brought them and others to the United States for plastic surgery and found them temporary homes in and near New York City – not an easy undertaking for the hosts in the Fifties when the word "peace" was almost a synonym for "Communism" and when many people had no desire to think about, not to say see with their own eyes, what American nuclear bombs had done to actual people. In fact, I could only guess at the results myself, as the two women were draped with veils of silk. I had an idea of faces partly melted. Through the Squires' guests I learned about the real meaning of war and nuclear weapons, and through the Squire family I had a sturdy idea of what it meant to conform one's life to the Gospel rather than to politics and the opinions of neighbors.

Yet the Methodist Church as such didn't excite me. While I prized Rev. Squire and enjoyed the jokes he sprinkled within sermons to underline his points, longtime sitting was hard work for a child. I felt no urge to be among those being baptized. Neither was I won over by the nearby Dutch Reformed Church which for some forgotten reason I attended for a few weeks or months and which I remember best for its unsuccessful attempt to get me to memorize the Ten Commandments.

The next big event in my religious development was thanks to a school friend inviting me to his church in the nearby town of Shrewsbury. It was among the oldest buildings in our region, its white clapboard scarred with musket balls fired with deadly purpose in the Revolutionary War. The blood of dying soldiers had stained the church's pews and floor, and though the stains could no longer be seen, it stirred me to think about what had happened there.

What engaged me still more was the form of worship, which was altar – rather than pulpit – centered. It was an Episcopal parish in which sacraments and ritual activity were the main events. (Being a parent has helped me realize that ritual is something that children naturally like; for all the experiments we make as children, we are born conservatives who want our parents to operate in predictable, patterned, reliable ways. We want meals to be on the table at a certain time and in a specific way, and in general like to know what to expect. We want the ordinary events of life to have what I think of now as liturgical shape.)

The parish was "high church" – vestments, acolytes, candles, processions, incense, liturgical seasons with their special colors, fast times, plain chant, communion every Sunday. I got a taste of a more ancient form of Christianity than I had found among Methodists. I loved it and for the first time in my life wanted not just to watch but to be part of it. It was in this church that, age nine or ten, I was baptized. I became an acolyte (thus getting to wear a bright red robe with crisp white surplice) and learned to assist the pastor, Father Lavant, at the altar. I learned much of the *Book of Common Prayer* by heart and rang a bell when the bread and wine were being consecrated. In Sunday school after the service I learned something of the history of Christianity, its sources and traditions, with much attention to Greek words. I remember Father Lavant writing eucharist on the blackboard, explaining it meant thanksgiving, and that it was made up of smaller Greek words that meant "well" and "grace." The eucharist was a well of grace. He was the sort of man who put the ancient world in reaching distance.

But the friendship which had brought me to the church in the first place disintegrated sometime that year. I no longer felt welcome in my friend's car, and felt awkward about coming to their church under my own steam, though it would have been possible to get there by bike.

Very likely the reason the car door no longer opened to me was political. My friend's parents probably became aware of our family's political color. Given the times, it would have been hard not to know.

I had little comprehension of the intense political pressures Americans were under, though I saw the same anti-communist films and television programs other kids saw and was painfully aware that my parents were "the enemy" – the people who were trying to subvert America, though I couldn't see a trace of this happening among the real live Communists I happened to know.

It was about that time that the FBI began to openly exhibit its interest in us, interviewing many of the neighbors. One day, while Mother was out, two FBI agents came into our house and finger-printed my brother and me. Such were the times.

My father's arrest in 1952 in St. Louis, where he was then living, was page one news across America. Dad faced the usual charge against Communists: "conspiracy to advocate the overthrow of the United States government by force and violence." I doubt many read this hair-raising assembly of phrases closely enough to notice that in fact the accused were not being charged with any violent or revolutionary actions or even with advocating such activities, but with being part of a *conspiracy* to advocate them.

The afternoon of Dad's arrest, my mother's brother drove up to our house, came to the door, and yelled at my mother while waving a newspaper that had a banner headline that said something like: TEN TOP REDS ARRESTED IN MISSOURI. He stormed off the porch, got back into his car, a black Buick, and drove away. I never saw my uncle again. Until then he had been a frequent visitor, though I was aware Mother took pains to avoid political topics when we were with him.

Dad was to spend half a year in prison before being bailed out. Several years passed before the charges against him were finally dropped.

While it was never nearly as bad for dissenters in the US as it was in the USSR – no gulag, no summary executions, no Stalin – nonetheless I have come to feel a sense of connection with the children of religious believers in Communist countries; they too know what it is like to have their parents vilified by the mass media and imprisoned by the government.

Though it was bad enough that Dad was in prison, I was still more aware of the pressures my mother was facing. The FBI had talked with her employers. Many Communists were losing or had lost their jobs; she took it for granted it would happen to her as well. This expectation was a factor in her not buying a car until well after my brother and I were full-grown, even though we lived pretty far off the beaten track. She took the bus to work and back again, or found colleagues who could give her a lift. When I pleaded with her to get a car, she explained we shouldn't develop needs that she might not be able to afford in the future.

Her only hope of keeping her job was to give her employers no hook on which to justify dismissal. Night after night for years she worked at her desk writing case histories of patients with whom she was involved. No matter how sick she might be, she never missed a day of work, never arrived late, never left early. I doubt that the State of New Jersey ever got more from an employee than they got from her. And it worked. She wasn't fired.

My religious interest went into recess. Within a year or two I was trying to make up my mind whether I was an atheist or an agnostic. I decided on the latter, because I couldn't dismiss the sense I often had of God being real. Like my parents, I loved nature, and nature is full of news about God. Wherever I looked, whether at ants with a magnifying glass or at the moon with a telescope, everything in the natural order was awe-inspiring, and awe is a religious state of mind. Creation made it impossible to dismiss God. But it was a rather impersonal God – God as prime mover rather than God among us.

It wasn't until 1959, when I was turning 18, that I began to think deeply about religion and what God might mean in my life.

At the turning point in his life, St. Paul was struck blind on the road to Damascus. The equivalent moment in my own life is linked to a more prosaic setting: Saturday night at the movies. Just out of Navy boot camp, I was studying meteorology at the Navy Weather School at Lakehurst, New Jersey. The film at the base theater happened to be *The Nun's Story*, based on the autobiography of a young Belgian who entered a convent and later worked at a missionary hospital in the African Congo. In the end, the nun (played by Audrey Hepburn) became an ex-nun. Conscience was at the heart of the story: conscience leading a young woman into the convent and eventually leading her elsewhere, but never away from her faith. I later discovered the film was much criticized in the Catholic press for its portrayal both of loneliness and of the abuse of authority in religious community.

If it had been Hollywood's usual religious movie of *The Bells of St. Mary's* variety, it would have had no impact on my life. But this was a true story, well acted and honestly told, and without a happy ending, though in the woman's apparent failure as a nun one found both integrity and faith. Against the rough surface of the story, I had a compelling glimpse of the Catholic Church with its rich and complex structures of worship and community.

After the film I went for a walk, heading away from the buildings and sidewalks. It was a warm, clear August evening. Gazing at the stars, I felt an uncomplicated and overwhelming happiness such as I had never known. This seemed to rise up through the grass and to shower down on me in the starlight. I felt I was floating on God's love like a leaf on water. I was deeply aware that everything that is or was or ever will be is joined together in God. For the first time in my life, the blackness beyond the stars wasn't terrifying.

I didn't think much about the film itself that night, except for a few words of Jesus that had been read to the novices during their first period of formation and which seemed to recite themselves within me as I walked: "If you would be perfect, go, sell what you have, and give it to the poor, and you will have great treasure in heaven, and come, follow me."

I went to sleep that night eager to go to Mass the next morning. I knew I wanted to be a Christian and was strongly drawn to Catholicism.

I went to a nearby Catholic church the next morning, but found the Mass disappointing. I felt like an anthropologist observing a strange tribal rite. I had only a vague idea what was happening. There seemed little connection between the priest and the congregation. Most of the worship was in mumbled, hurried, automatic Latin, except for the sermon, which perhaps I would have preferred had it been in Latin. People in the pews seemed either bored or were concentrating on their rosaries. At least they knew when to sit, stand, and kneel. I struggled awkwardly to keep up with them. At the end of Mass, there was no exchange of greetings or further contact between people who had been praying together. Catholic worship seemed to have all the intimacy of supermarket shopping.

Still resolved to become a Christian, I started looking for a church where there was engagement and beauty and at least something of what I had hoped to find in Catholicism. The Anglo-Catholic segment of the Episcopal Church, which I had begun to know as a child, seemed the obvious choice, and it happened that another sailor at the Weather School had been part of a high church parish. He shared his *Book of Common Prayer* with me and in the weeks that followed we occasionally read its services of morning and evening prayer together.

After graduating, I spent a two-week Christmas leave in an Episcopal monastery on the Hudson River, a joyous experience in which I thought I had found everything I was hoping for in the Catholic Church: liturgy, the sacraments, and a religious community that combined prayer, study, and service. Stationed with a Navy unit at the Weather Bureau in Washington, DC, I joined a local high church Episcopal parish, St. Paul's, which the monks had told me about.

Those months were full of grace. So why am I not writing an essay on "Why I am an Episcopalian"? One piece of the answer is that I had never quite let go of the Catholic Church. I could never walk past a Catholic church without stopping in to pray. A hallmark of the Catholic

Church was that the Blessed Sacrament was reserved on or near the altar awaiting anyone who came in. Its presence meant this wasn't just a room that came to life from time to time but a place where many of the curtains that usually hide God were lifted, even if you were the only person present. The doors of Catholic churches always seemed open.

Another factor were the books that found their way into my hands, especially Thomas Merton's autobiography, *The Seven Storey Mountain*, G.K. Chesterton's *Orthodoxy*, and *The Long Loneliness* by Dorothy Day, the founder of the Catholic Worker movement.

There were negative elements as well. One of these was an experience at the Episcopal monastery I occasionally visited. On the last day of an Easter stay one of the monks asked to see me. Once in the visiting room, he pulled me into a closet and embraced me. I struggled free and left the monastery in great confusion. Back in Washington, I wrote to the prior of the community, telling him what had happened. His reply wasn't helpful. He might have pointed out that monks, like everyone else, suffer loneliness and have sexual longings of one sort or another and sometimes don't manage them very well. Rather he said that homosexuality was often an indication of a monastic vocation. As my own sexual orientation was of the more common variety, I wondered if the prior meant I wasn't the right sort of person to be visiting. After his letter, I had no desire to return. The experience underscored my growing doubts about remaining in the Episcopal Church.

Yet I still had reservations about becoming Catholic and so began to explore the varieties of Christianity in Washington, visiting every sort of church, black and white, high and low. Among them was a Greek Orthodox cathedral, but it seemed a cool, unwelcoming place; I sensed one had to be Greek to be a part of it. I returned several times to the black church on the campus of Howard University, which was a friendly place with wonderful singing, but felt that, as a white person, I would always be an outsider. If I could have changed skin color by wishing, I would have turned black in the Howard chapel.

As the weeks passed I came to realize that the Catholic churches I visited were places in which I felt an at-homeness I hadn't found elsewhere. On November 26, 1960, after several months of instruction, I was received into the Catholic Church.

What had most attracted me to Catholicism was the liturgy. Though in some parishes it was a dry, mechanical affair, there were other parishes where the care taken in every aspect of worship was profound. While for some people worship in an ancient language is a barrier, in my own case I came to love the Latin. I was happy to be participating in a language of worship that was being used simultaneously in every part of the world and which also was a bridge of connection with past generations. I learned many Latin prayers by heart, especially anything that could be sung, and still sing Latin prayers and hymns. "To sing is to pray twice," one of the Church Fathers says. How true!

In the early stages of liturgical revision that followed the Second Vatican Council, I felt a complex mixture of expectation and anxiety. Despite my private love of the language, I could hardly disagree with the many arguments put forward for scrapping Latin. I didn't want to hang onto what apparently got in the way for others.

The Englishing of the Liturgy was, unfortunately, not carried out by poets but seemed to be committee work. We ended up with language in its flattest state. We lost not only Latin but Gregorian chant and this too was, in my view, a pity. Most of the music that took its place was pedestrian at every level, fit for shopping malls and Disneyland. The sand blasting had also removed incense. The body language of prayer was in retreat. The holy water fonts were dry. Many bridges linking body and soul were abandoned.

Yet, again like most Catholics, I uttered few if any words of complaint. I knew that change is not a comfortable experience. And I thought of myself as a modern person; I was embarrassed by my difficulties adjusting to change. Also I had no sense of connection with those who were protesting change. These tended to be the rigid Catholics of the sort who object to Catholics having contact with Protestants. (I had never been attracted to that icy wing of Catholicism that argued one must be a Catholic, and a most obedient Catholic, in order to be saved.)

If one has experienced only the modern "fast-food" liturgy of the Catholic Church, perhaps the typical modern Mass isn't so disappointing. But for me there was a deep sense of loss. For years I usually left church feeling depressed.

All this said, there was a positive side to Catholicism that in many ways compensated for what was missing in the Liturgy. For all its problems and inner tensions, which no church is without, the Catholic Church has the strength of being a world community in which many members see themselves as being on the same footing as fellow Catholics on the other side of the globe; in contrast many Orthodox Christians see their church, even Christ, primarily in national terms. The Catholic Church also possesses a strong sense of co-responsibility for the social order, and a relatively high degree of independence from all political and economic structures.

This aspect of the Catholic Church finds expression in many structures. I joined one of these, the Catholic Worker movement, after receiving a conscientious objector discharge from the Navy in 1960.

Founded by Dorothy Day in 1933, the Catholic Worker has become well known for its "houses of hospitality" _ places of welcome in run-down urban areas where those in need can receive food, clothing, and shelter. It is a movement not unlike the early Franciscans, attempting to live out the Gospels in a simple, literal way. Jesus urged us to be poor; those involved in the Catholic Worker struggle to have as little as possible. Jesus said to do good to and pray for those who curse you, to love your enemies, to put away the sword; and Catholic Workers try to do this as well, refusing to take part in war or violence. The Catholic Worker view of the world is no less critical than that of the Prophets and the Gospel. There was a remarkable interest in the writings of the Church Fathers. One often found quotations from St. John Chrysostom, St. Gregory Nazianzen, Saint Basil, and other voices of the early Church in the movement's widely read publication, *The Catholic Worker*.

I found in Dorothy Day not only an awareness of the Eastern Church but a profound love of its richness and way of worship. She also had a special love for Russian literature, especially the writings of Dostoevsky. At times she recited passages from *The Brothers Karamazov* that had shaped her understanding of Christianity; mainly these had to do with the saintly *staretz*, Father Zosima (a figure modeled in part on the *staretz* Father Amvrosi who was canonized by the Russian Church in 1988), and his teaching on active love. Dorothy inspired me to read Dostoevsky. It was Dorothy who first took me into a Russian Orthodox Church, a cathedral in upper Manhattan where I met a priest who, a quarter century later, I was to meet again in Moscow, Father Matvay Stadniuk. (In 1988 he launched the first public project of voluntary service by Church members since Soviet power had launched its war on religion.) At a liturgy she took me to I first learned to sing the Old Slavonic words, *"Gospodi pomiloi"* -- Lord have mercy -- the main prayer of Orthodoxy.

One evening Dorothy brought me to a Manhattan apartment for a meeting of the Third Hour, a Christian ecumenical group founded by a Russian émigré, Helene Iswolsky. The conversation was in part about the Russian word for spirituality, *dukhovnost*. The Russian understanding of spiritual life, it was explained, not only suggests a private relationship between the praying person and God but has profound social content: moral capacity, social responsibility, courage, wisdom, mercy, a readiness to forgive, a way of life centered in love. Much of the discussion flew over my head. At times I was more attentive to the remarkable face of the poet W.H. Auden, a member of the Third Hour group. I recall talk about *iurodivi*, the "holy fools" who revealed Christ in ways that would be regarded as insanity in the west, and *stralniki*, those who wandered Russia in continuous pilgrimage, begging for bread and reciting with every breath and step the silent prayer, "Lord Jesus Christ, Son of the God, have mercy on me, a sinner."

One of the people Dorothy was in touch with was the famous Trappist monk and author, Thomas Merton, whose autobiography, *The Seven Storey Mountain*, had been a factor in my becoming a Catholic. Through Dorothy I came to be one of his correspondents and later his guest at the Abbey of Our Lady of Gethsemani in Kentucky. Besides many letters, Merton used to send me photographs of Russian and Greek icons. Icons had played an important part in his conversion to Christianity and, as I was to discover in writing a book about him, in his continuing spiritual life.

Thanks to Merton and Dorothy Day, I was more aware than many western Christians of the Eastern Church, but Orthodoxy seemed to me more an ethnic club than a place for an American with a family tree whose roots stretched from Ireland to the Urals, more a living museum than a living Church. My eyes were slow in opening to icons. While the music in Russian churches was amazingly beautiful, Orthodox services seemed too long and the ritual too ornate. I was in a typical American hurry about most things, even worship, and had the usual American aversion to trimmings. Orthodoxy seemed excessive.

As much of my adult life has been spent editing peace movement publications, one might imagine such work would have opened many East-West doors for me. Ironically, however, through most of the Cold War the peace movement in the United States was notable for its avoidance of contact with the Soviet Union. Perhaps because we were so routinely accused of being "tools of the Kremlin," peace activists tended to steer clear of the USSR and rarely knew more about it than anyone else. Even to visit the Soviet Union was to be convicted of everything the *Reader's Digest* had ever said about KGB direction of peace groups in the West.

In the spring of 1982, after five years of living in Holland while heading the staff of the International Fellowship of Reconciliation, I was on a speaking trip that took me to twenty American cities. At the time the Nuclear Freeze movement was gathering strength. It advocated a bilateral end to nuclear testing, freezing the manufacture of nuclear weapons, and halting development of new weapons systems. Millions of people, both Democratic and Republican, supported the Freeze. Yet I came back to Holland convinced that its prospects for success were slight. The Freeze, like many peace campaigns during the Cold War, was built mainly on fear of nuclear weapons. Practically nothing was being done to respond to relationship issues or fear of the Soviet Union. All that was needed was one nasty incident to burst the balloon, and that came when a Soviet pilot shot down a South Korean 747 passenger plane flying across Soviet air space. The image of the west facing a barbaric and ruthless enemy was instantly revived. The Freeze movement crashed with the 747 jet.

The trip brought home to me that both in the peace movement and in the military, we in the West knew more about weapons than the people at whom the weapons were aimed. I began to look for an opportunity to travel in the Soviet Union.

At the time it wasn't easy to find an opening. The Soviet Union was at war in Afghanistan, an event sharply condemned by the organization I was working for. A seminar we had arranged in Moscow was abruptly canceled on the Soviet side. An editor of *Izvestia* whom I met in Amsterdam candidly explained that there was apprehension in the Kremlin of pacifists from the West unveiling protest signs in Red Square.

In October 1983, a few representatives of the International Fellowship of Reconciliation met several leaders of the Christian Peace Conference for a dialogue on the subject of "Violence, Nonviolence and Liberation." We met in Moscow in an old wooden building used at that time by the External Church Affairs Department of the Russian Orthodox Church.

The meeting would have been useful no matter where it had happened. But for me it had an unexpected spiritual significance simply because it was in Russia. I experienced a particular sense of connection with the Russian Orthodox believers and longed to have the chance for more prolonged contact.

A year later I was back in Moscow for another meeting. The discussion this time was less engaging – the exchange (sadly not dialogue) was mainly with hard-line Communists in the Soviet Peace Committee. For me the primary significance of the trip was the contact with Orthodox believers.

The high point was participation in the liturgy at the Epiphany Cathedral. This isn't one of the city's oldest or most beautiful churches, though it has an outstanding choir. The icons, coming from the eighteenth and nineteenth centuries, were a far cry from Rublev and Theofan the Greek. And yet being in that throng of devout worshippers was a more illuminating experience than I have had in far more beautiful churches. The place became beautiful for me simply because it was such a grace to be there.

The church was crowded as a church in the West would be only on a major feast day. As is usual in the Russian Orthodox Church, there were no pews. There were a few benches and chairs along the walls for those who needed them, but I found it freeing to be on my feet. Though at times it was uncomfortable to be standing up for so long, being upright helped make me more attentive. It was like a move from the bleachers to the field. (I'd like one day to learn how chairs and benches made their way into churches. Is it connected with the Reformation's recentering of services around the sermon? Perhaps it happened when people got bored.)

I was fascinated by the linking together of spiritual and physical activity. Making the sign of the cross and half bows were ordinary elements of prayer. Orthodox believers seemed to cross themselves and bow almost continually. I was reminded of the patterns the wind makes blowing across a field of wheat as I watched the rippling of bowing heads in the tightly packed congregation.

All the while the most beautiful singing was going on, mainly from two choirs facing each other in balconies on either side of the huge cupola. For the Creed and Our Father, the congregation joined with the choirs, singing with great force.

At first I stood like a statue, though wanting to do what those around me were doing. It seemed so appropriate for an incarnational religion to link body and soul through these simple gestures. It must have taken me most of an hour before I began to pray in the Russian style.

The sense of people being deeply at prayer was as tangible as Russian black bread. I felt that if the walls and pillars of the church were taken away, the roof would rest securely on the prayers of the congregation below. I have very rarely experienced this kind of intense spiritual presence. In its intensity, though there are many superficial differences, I can only compare it to the black church in America.

The experience led me to write *Pilgrim to the Russian Church*, a book which required a number of Russian trips; on one of these I was joined by my wife, Nancy.

In the course of my travels I came to love the slow, unhurried tradition of prayer in Orthodoxy, deeply appreciating its absent-mindedness about the clock. The liturgy rarely started on time, never ended on time, and lasted two or three hours, still longer on great feasts. I discovered that Orthodox believers are willing to give to worship the kind of time and devotion that Italians give to their evening meals.

I became increasingly aware of how deep and mindful is Orthodox preparation for communion, with special stress on forgiveness of others as a precondition for reception of the sacrament.

I enjoyed watching confession in Orthodox churches. The penitent and priest weren't tucked away in closets but stood in front on the iconostasis, faces nearly touching. There is a tenderness about it that never ceases to amaze me. (While I still don't find confession easy, I don't envy those forms of Christianity that do without it.)

I quickly came to appreciate Orthodoxy for taking literally Jesus's teaching, "Let the children come to me and hinder them not." In our Catholic parish in Holland, our daughter Anne had gone from confusion and hurt to pain and anger after many attempts to receive communion with Nancy and me. She hadn't reached "the age of reason" and therefore couldn't receive the instruction considered a prerequisite to sacramental life. But a child in an Orthodox parish is at the front of the line to receive communion.

I came to esteem the married clergy of Orthodoxy. While there are many Orthodox monks and nuns, and celibacy is an honored state, marriage is more valued in Orthodoxy than Catholicism. Sexual discipline is taken seriously, yet one isn't left feeling that the main sins are sexual.

I came to cherish the relative darkness that is usual in Orthodox churches, where the main light source is candles. Candle light encourages a climate of intimacy. Icons are intended for candle light.

Praying with icons was an aspect of Orthodox spirituality that opened its doors to us even though we weren't yet Orthodox. During a three-month sabbatical in 1985 when we were living near Jerusalem, we bought a small Russian icon of Mary and Jesus and began praying before it. It proved to be a school of prayer. We learned much about prayer by simply standing in front of our icon.

All the while Nancy and I were continuing our frustrating search for a Catholic parish that we could be fully a part of in our Dutch town.

On the one hand there were parishes that seemed connected to the larger Church only by frayed threads; parishes were abandoning rituals, traditions and lines of connection which seemed to us worth preserving, and going their own way. There were other parishes that, in ritual life, were clearly part of a larger Church but where there was no sense of welcome or warmth.

Finally Nancy and I became part of a parish where, by joining the choir, we felt more a part of a church community. But we were far and away the youngest members of the choir and still felt quite apart. None of our children were willing to come.

How we envied Russian Orthodox believers! Oddly enough it didn't occur to me that there might be a similar quality of worship in Orthodox churches in the West. I thought that Orthodoxy was like certain wines that must be sipped at the vineyard. I also had the idea that Russian parishes in the West must be filled with bitter refugees preoccupied with hating Communists.

Then in January 1988, at the invitation of Father Alexis Voogd, pastor of the St. Nicholas of Myra church in Amsterdam, Nancy and I took part in a special ecumenical service to mark the beginning of the Russian Orthodox Church's Millennium celebration: a thousand years since the baptism of the citizens of Kiev. Catholics, Protestants and Orthodox, we were packed into the tiny church for a service that was a hodge-podge of speeches by clergy from various local churches interspersed with beautiful Russian hymns sung by the parish choir.

If it was just that ecumenical service, perhaps, we might not have returned. But at the reception in the parish hall that followed, we were startled to experience a kind of interaction that I had rarely found in any church in any country, not to say in prudent, understated Holland.

Walking to the train station afterward, we decided to come back and see what the liturgy was like in Amsterdam. The following Sunday we discovered it was every bit as profound as it was in Russia. And that was that. We managed only once or twice to return to mass in our former parish. Before a month had passed we realized that a prayer we had been living with a long time had been answered: we had found a church we wholeheartedly could belong to and couldn't bear *not* going to even if it meant getting out of bed early and traveling by train and tram to Amsterdam every week.

On Palm Sunday 1988, I was received into the Orthodox Church; Nancy made the same step on Pentecost.

In many ways it wasn't such a big step from where we had been. Orthodoxy and Catholicism have so much in common: sacraments, apostolic succession, the calendar of feasts and fasts, devotion to the Mother of God, and much more. Yet in Orthodoxy we found an even deeper sense of connection with the early Church and a far more vital form of liturgical life. Much that has been neglected in Catholicism and abandoned in Protestant churches, especially confession and fasting, remain central in Orthodox life. We quickly found what positive, life-renewing gifts they were, and saw that they were faring better in a climate that was less legalistic but more demanding.

A postscript: The religious movement in my life, which from the beginning was influenced by my parents, also influenced them. While neither followed me into Catholicism or Orthodoxy, in the early Sixties my mother returned to the Methodist Church and remains much a part of her church to this day; she had resigned from the Communist Party at the time the Soviets put down the Hungarian uprising. Despite her age and failing eyesight, she continues in her struggle for the poor, much to the consternation of local politicians and bureaucrats. While my father never left "the Party" (to the end of his life he wore rose-colored glasses when looking at the USSR), he eventually became a Unitarian. He enjoyed the joke about Unitarians believing *at most* in one God. In the last two decades of his life he was especially active in developing low-income and inter-racial housing projects in California. A cooperative he helped found in Santa Rosa was singled out for several honors, including the Certificate of National Merit from the US Department of Housing and Urban

Development. He was always deeply supportive of my religious commitment, and I recall with particular happiness hearing him reading aloud to my step-mother from my book, *Pilgrim to the Russian Church*. On his death bed in the spring of 1990, he borrowed the crucifix I normally wear around my neck. It was in his hands when he died.

Jim Forest is co-secretary of the Orthodox Peace Fellowship and editor of Peace Media Service. He is a former General Secretary of the International Fellowship of Reconciliation. His books include Religion in the New Russia, Pilgrim to the Russian Church, Love is the Measure: A Biography of Dorothy Day, and Living with Wisdom: a Life of Thomas Merton. He has lived in the Netherlands since 1977 and is a member of the St. Nicholas of Myra Russian Orthodox Church in Amsterdam.

Come Let Us Worship:
My Journey to Orthodoxy
by Sister Verna Harrison

At Dwight Chapel on the Old Campus of Yale University on April 14, 1974, in the wee hours of the morning, there was a joyous party. The congregation of the Episcopal chaplaincy was celebrating Easter with a festive meal, and we joined hands in a circle and danced, singing, "Christ is risen from the dead, trampling down death by death, and upon those in the tombs bestowing life!" I was a particularly enthusiastic participant. We had just finished a glorious Paschal vigil service, in a modified Episcopalian rite incorporating some hymns and much of the spirit of the Orthodox rite, and I was baptized during that service.[7]

I was a senior at Yale at the time. During my college years, where I pursued a double major in philosophy and political science, with emphasis on political theory, I wondered how the quality of human existence could be improved, and like many people in those days looked for answers in the realm of politics. But my studies of skeptical philosophers such as Nietzsche had undercut the foundations of the humanistic ethical system in which I had believed, and I was discontented with the skepticism. I wanted to reject Hitler's actions, for example, as evil, but found I had no objective criteria by which to do so. Meanwhile, I was quite discouraged about the prospects for political change that would bring significant improvement in the world. At the same time, in some vague way, I felt that there was something wrong in my personal existence, and that I needed a change in my life.

At home, I had been taught that religion was a matter of faith. Some people had it, others didn't, and we were among the ones who didn't. It was like a kind of hobby, perhaps, like fishing or knitting, which some

---

7   The Orthodox Church does not perform baptisms during the midnight Paschal service, but mine somehow approximated what that might be like, if it were possible. It was surely among the most momentous days of my life. On every Pascha I find I am celebrating my spiritual birthday as well as Christ's Feast of Feasts.

people fancied but not others. Still, I was taught always to treat other people's faith with respect.

My father, an engineer for whom the quest for truth meant a scrupulous objectivity in taking account of all the scientific evidence, has described himself as a benign agnostic, and this label would fit most of my relatives pretty well, including those who consider themselves atheists.[8] A man of great kindness and integrity, he taught me the importance of always looking for truth, which I took very much to heart, and he spoke with reverence about Socrates. But from an early age, in a childlike way, I understood the need to seek truth in a much more total and ultimate sense.

In hindsight, I realize that I was never truly satisfied with agnosticism, although it did not occur to me to question it until I'd had three and a half years of liberal education at Yale. As a child I had a great longing for authentic goodness and justice and did not know where to find it. I needed a kind, patient teacher who would encourage and guide me through all my mistakes so that I could learn, a little at a time. Unfortunately, during childhood I did not have such a teacher of moral life. However, my parents and teachers did encourage me in school, and I did very well in academic work.

As a child I also wanted to ask theological questions, though I could not conceptualize them as such, and remember a series of animated discussions in class about whether who and what we are is determined more by heredity or environment. I kept thinking that our identities as human beings must have some other cause as well, that whatever it is must be important, and that heredity and environment could not explain everything. But when at last I dared to suggest that there must be another factor involved, everybody laughed, and I did not venture to bring it up again. Yet I continued to ask, "Why am I me and not someone else?" I lacked the vocabulary but wondered what accounted for the mystery of human personhood. In physics and astronomy, I wondered about the origins of the universe, and in mathematics I was fascinated with different kinds of infinity.

---

8   They have been, however, admirably supportive of me in my decisions to become a Christian, study theology, join the Orthodox Church, and enter monastic life. Though they do not pray themselves, they sometimes ask me to pray for their loved ones. I am thankful for this, especially since I know that others who make similar decisions are not always blessed with such approval from family members.

by Sister Verna Harrison

At the beginning of the spring semester of my senior year at Yale, when it finally occurred to me to wonder about God, I thought, "I am an agnostic and don't know whether or not God exists. That means maybe he does, and if so I'd better do something about it." I also thought, "If God exists, miracles are possible, because he can do anything."

On February 4, 1974, I suddenly felt, with considerable fear and trembling, that I might be in God's presence. If so, I had to come to terms with him somehow. I decided to try praying and going to church and see if anything happened. It was an experiment in which I really had nothing to lose except a little time and effort. If nothing happened, I did not have to continue, but I was determined to give it an honest try. I went to see a friend in the dorm, a devout Roman Catholic, and talked with him until the early hours of the morning. For the next three or four days, I went to early morning masses with him at a local parish church.

It was sleepy and uneventful. I knelt in the back of the church and prayed that God would give me faith and teach me to pray. My friend would leave me there and go up to receive communion. About the third morning, an Irish priest gave a sermon, saying that we should not only ask God to give us things we want, we should also pray, "Do with me as you will." So I added this to my requests for faith and an understanding of prayer.

It did not take long for something to happen. On the morning after that late night conversation, I felt that my whole perception of reality was changed. I remember walking along the street a block from my dorm and seeing that everything looked incredibly brilliant and beautiful. The little specks of pebble or glass in the sidewalk beneath my feet shone like diamonds. I had the sense that God was present everywhere and that he was watching me all the time. I did not have the vocabulary to describe it, but what I saw was a glimpse of the world transfigured.

This sense of being in his presence continued. For those few days, it was truly frightening. To me it meant one of two things. Either I was going crazy, or God was real and I urgently needed to be on good terms with him. On that first evening, February 4th, I had also spoken to another acquaintance in the dorm, John RePass, an evangelical and a member of the Christian Fellowship. Several months previously he had spoken to me about Christ and, as I always did on such occasions, I had told him politely that I was not interested. He told me that if I ever decided I was interested, he would be happy to talk again.

I went to see him and we spoke briefly. At the end of the week, after four days of my fearful sense of presence and transfiguration, I decided that the experience was real and I was not crazy, so I had to make a commitment to God, though I was not sure how. John took me to see two other neighbors who explained to me that what I needed to do was accept Jesus Christ as my Lord and Savior and give my life to him. I reflected on what had happened during that week and how I had prayed, "Do with me as you will," and I told them solemnly that I had already done this. They were overjoyed, thanked the Lord, and immediately became my friends.[9] I sought to find out about everything Christian and make it part of my life. I became involved in the Yale Christian Fellowship, a branch of the Inter-Varsity group. I participated regularly in their activities, except that once a year when they had to elect officers I did not vote. The reason was that there was a statement of faith one had to sign. Everything in it basically came from the Nicene Creed, which I gladly believed, except one part that affirmed the inerrancy of Scripture. In effect, this was part of their Creed. Since I could not accept it, I would not sign.

In April, 1991 at a conference on St. Gregory the Theologian at Holy Cross Greek Orthodox Seminary, Frederick Norris[10] presented a paper saying that, according to Gregory, the Bible as a whole is the inspired Word of God, but it contains occasional errors in matters of detail. I realized that he was articulating a view of Scripture close to the view I had held since I first became a Christian. Of course, this is a late 20th century description of Patristic exegesis. Gregory himself and the other Fathers would have said rather that every word in the Bible is divinely inspired, but that in some places it can be understood as true only in a spiritual, not in a literal sense. They took care to interpret Scripture ecclesially, theologically, and pastorally, in ways that agree with the teaching of the Church, are morally worthy of God, and help people toward salvation. As skilled physicians of souls, they realized that the same spiritual medicine could heal one person and harm another, so a

---

9   John RePass also figures in a later part of this story. He became Orthodox quite independently of me. Now he is a hieromonk at St. Tikhon's Monastery, where he has been for some years, and his name is Father Juvenaly.

10   Frederick W. Norris is Professor of Theology at Emmanuel School of Religion in Johnson City, Tennessee and a leading expert on St. Gregory the Theologian. Currently, in 1993-94, he is President of the North American Patristic Society, the professional organization for scholars specializing in early Christianity. He is also a fine colleague and a friend.

wise and discerning application of the inspired words is essential. I now accept this Orthodox approach to the Bible wholeheartedly.[11]

That first Sunday after I had committed myself to becoming a Christian, I went with one of the students to a Baptist service. There did not seem to be much to it -- a rather uninspiring sermon and two or three hymns. That same evening, John RePass took me to the liturgy of the Episcopal Church at Yale, although he did not go there regularly himself. It was a beautiful Eucharist, sung a cappella, with some hymnography borrowed from the Orthodox, and I immediately fell in love with it. When I learned that they did it six days a week, I went every day (except Saturday, their day off). Within a few weeks, I started to experience moments of ineffable joy and sweetness in my personal prayers as well. After my baptism, I continued this practice for as long as I was at Yale. After the service, the students would go to dinner together. They accepted me immediately and some of them became my closest friends. This happy time in my life was to be brief. I graduated in June and in the fall went to Oxford to study political philosophy and theory. When I got there I realized that all my interest in this subject had dried up and blown away over the summer. I had no motivation and could not go on. After arranging to take a year's leave and start again the next fall, I went back to New Haven. It was a welcome sabbatical after years of intense study, and I needed to assimilate the changes that had occurred so rapidly and decide what to do next. I attended the Episcopal services for another academic year, went to the Christian Fellowship meetings, read theological books, and prayed a lot. During this time I also learned the Jesus prayer from one of the Episcopal chaplains and made retreats at two or three monastic communities, where the way of life fascinated, as well as frightened, me.

By spring I realized that if I tried to begin with political science again at Oxford I would have no more motivation than I'd had the first time. I reapplied to study philosophy and theology and because of my previous acceptance was readmitted. I returned in the fall of 1975 to a different college and a different course of studies. A few weeks into my first term I switched to straight theology, where my academic focus has remained. I stayed for two years and earned my M.A.

---

11   When I was received into the Orthodox Church, I had to accept a statement of faith saying that I would interpret Scripture in accordance with the teaching of the Fathers. I was comfortable with this as I was never comfortable with fundamentalist or conservative Protestant doctrines of inerrancy, even when I associated with those groups for the sake of prayer and Christian fellowship.

Oxford is a wonderful place to be a devout young Anglican. Every college has its chapel, and there are additional Christian student groups as well as parishes in the town. All kinds of churchmanship are represented, from low to high, from evangelical to Anglo-Catholic. I attended quite a few of these churches during my two years there, but with a preference for the more liturgical kind. My practice was to go to church twice a day and also to evangelical meetings. My Episcopalianism gave me the flexibility to explore all kinds of Christian spirituality, which I needed to do at the time.

For the first few years after my initial conversion I was engaged in sorting out which aspects of Christianity I wanted to incorporate into my life and pursue further. I tried various things. Some led to dead ends that prevented me from moving closer to God, and in time I gave them up. Evangelicalism eventually brought me to such a dead end.

What I learned from the evangelicals was that I can and should have a personal relationship with our Lord Jesus Christ, that I can pray to him at any time in my own words about everything that concerns me, and that he is always present and will listen. This kind of prayer and relationship with him have been central to me since the beginning of my Christian life and continue to be so. But my major frustration was that the evangelicals generally did not carry this personal relationship far enough. When I heard preachers exhorting people to accept Christ as their Lord and Savior and give their lives to him, in my heart I found I wanted to do so, not only once as they taught, but over and over, every day even. The personal relationship was stressed at the beginning of one's conversion, but later the emphasis was on Bible reading and the teachings of church leaders, not one's own experience. In appearance at least, what was given with one hand was taken away with the other. Church attendance and Bible study could become routine, and there was not nearly enough prayer and worship. In my search to deepen my personal relationship with the Lord, I had to look elsewhere.

However, in Oxford my quest first led me to become involved in the charismatic movement. The charismatics I knew sought to practice unceasing prayer, openness to the will of God in every moment, and continual praise and thanksgiving to our Lord. They taught that Christ is present in all the events of daily life and can act wondrously and disclose his truth and will to us at any time. Yet alongside this emphasis on God's closeness and self-disclosure, they had great devotion to the mystery and unknowability of God. The practice of prayer in unknown tongues enabled us to carry our adoration of God beyond the reach of our own understanding. Though it is different in many ways, in this respect it somehow comes close to Orthodox prayer of the heart, which brings one into a profound encounter with God as unknowable. The charismatics had a sense that we live intimately with one who is incomprehensible and loves us very much. The only appropriate response is one of faith, adoration, thanksgiving, openness, surrender and obedience. All this brought me great joy.

The problem was that the context in which it was practiced was unstable, and the charismatics lacked authentic criteria of spiritual discernment. In time I found that fundamentalism, sexism, and authoritarianism were the three main dangers. I wanted to obey the Holy Spirit, but I did not see why this meant I should obey the group's leader. There were no yardsticks for assessing supposedly divine directives except the opinion of the leader or of the group as a whole. Yet it was impossible to participate in the spiritual practice except by approaching it with openness and receptivity. This also made critical evaluation difficult.

Following my time in Oxford, I went to Nashville, Tennessee for a year. After several months there, I told one of the group's assistant leaders in confidence that I did not believe in the inerrancy of Scripture. He revealed this confidence to the group, which went on to criticize me, and he claimed that the Holy Spirit had led him to do this. The chief pastor told me my main spiritual problem was that I needed to learn submission to authority. A couple of weeks after this, he issued a prophesy to me in front of the whole group. It began, "Why do you persist in rebelling against me and wallowing in self-pity?" These words were so painful and shocking that I could not assimilate or remember the rest of what was said. I was stunned. For about 24 hours I feared that Christ might really be hostile to me, as expressed in this utterance. Then I realized that the loving Lord I knew had never treated me in such a manner, and that the prophesy came not from him but from the group leader. After this I could not continue in the charismatic movement. When I understood that I could not be sure which messages came from the Holy Spirit and which did not, I was unable to maintain the openness needed to participate in this kind of prayer.

Why was worship without submission to authority impossible? It is only within the past three years, since I began my monastic commitment, that I think I have come to some understanding of the reason for this.

As I moved toward embracing monastic life, I found that more and more my prayer involved going out beyond my understanding into the unknowable and with love immersing myself in the divine mystery. But if God is incomprehensible, his wisdom and will for me are somehow included in this incomprehensibility. I also affirm that God's truth and will are revealed abundantly in the Orthodox Church. Yet increasingly I have come to recognize the importance of the apophatic as well as the kataphatic dimension in spirituality. [12]There needs to be a balance in which what is known and what is beyond the knowable are both acknowledged in prayer and life as well as in theological conceptualization. As my apophatic prayer grew deeper, it needed to be expressed, actualized, and carried further through an apophatic way of living and acting. This required a renunciation of my own will and understanding that I could practice daily in specific concrete actions. My heart longed for greater openness, submission, and obedience to the holy will of God, knowing that these are inseparable from more profound worship.

My monastic commitment has proven to be what most helps to fulfill this longing, although at the same time the longing itself only becomes greater. Every day I follow a prescribed rule of prayer and obey some other directives regarding dress, diet, etc. My experience is that the obedience I give to my spiritual father by doing these things has a sacramental quality. It provides a very direct and unambiguous way of giving certain of my actions to Christ. Yet let me emphasize that this is God's gift to me much more than it is something I do. It brings me deeper prayer, immense joy, and increased spiritual freedom.

Oddly enough, I have rediscovered something I had found in an intermittent and unstable way in my earlier charismatic experience. I find that worship of the unknowable in God goes together with obedience.

---

12   Apophatic theology acknowledges the radical transcendence of God by stating what He is not, by saying that He is unlike anything in the created universe. Apophatic spirituality involves an awareness of God precisely as unknowable in which He is encountered and experienced not as someone absent or as an intellectual abstraction but as the living God. Kataphatic theology affirms, articulates, and confesses the positive Orthodox beliefs that God has revealed about Himself through Scripture and Tradition. In kataphatic spirituality, this confession of faith becomes a confession of praise. In the life of the Church, all these approaches to theology and spirituality are needed. They are present together and support each other.

Going beyond intellect also means renunciation of one's own will. So perhaps there was an authentic spiritual reason why the charismatic groups tended to become authoritarian. The followers must have discovered they needed to practice submission, and the leaders provided it, though they had no context or training to help them provide it in a healthy way. Unfortunately, under these conditions unhealthy and even abusive psychological dynamics could easily occur in the groups. What they lacked was Holy Tradition and the guidance of wise and humble spiritual fathers.

The Orthodox Church provides a whole context of teaching and practice that shows how and within what limits pastoral authority is to be exercised. Since there are no criteria by which to assess authority in fundamentalist or charismatic groups, the leader's decision becomes the only criterion. They have the Bible, of course, but when isolated from its proper context in the Church it can be interpreted any number of ways. This can lead to all kinds of imbalance, theological error, spiritual delusion, and emotional abuse. (Tragically, this can happen in Orthodox fringe groups and unhealthy monasteries as well.) In Orthodoxy, the apophatic mystery is balanced by the enormous wealth of divine self-disclosure in Scripture, patristic writings, canons, dogma, iconography, and liturgy. Obedience in this context can be healthy because it occurs within the specific limits delineated by Orthodoxy of teaching and practice, and is balanced by the conciliarity of bishops, pastors, and the whole Church. Nobody rightly has absolute authority or is considered infallible. In my experience, knowing that I am called to obey certain persons in specified ways frees me from the pressure to obey whoever wants to place demands on me as an expression of "Christian love." My obligation has become more focused and defined and thus more manageable. So I have greater freedom instead of a greater burden.

Another weakness of the charismatic movement I knew was that going beyond intellect into the divine mystery often meant the suppression of intellect as well. This led to fundamentalism and blindness in the practice of submission. In contrast, Orthodoxy affirms the intellect within its own sphere of operation as well as going beyond it. The Church has an immensely rich theological heritage, which we are called to learn consciously and to appropriate personally, using our best reasoning abilities. Our task is to worship God with all our human faculties, with the body and the senses in liturgical worship, but also with the mind.

Apophatic prayer leads me beyond or above reason, not against it. It involves a union of mind and heart, not a replacement of one by the other. Moreover, I have found that my appreciation of God's mystery and my theological understanding of his self-manifestation reinforce each other and increase together. Similarly, in practicing obedience, I find I have not given up my own freedom or responsibility. Instead I am given some better tools to help me use them well. Orthodoxy teaches that we are to move toward wholeness within ourselves so that more and more we can offer the whole of ourselves to Christ. This could not happen if we had to use some of our human faculties to deny or suppress others.

As a student at Oxford, I had the opportunity to experience Anglican worship at its best and in great variety, which was a joy. But beginning in my first term I also became acquainted with the Orthodox. My two Episcopal chaplains at Yale had both studied in England and become acquainted with Orthodoxy there, and I first learned of it from them. When I went there myself to study, therefore, they told me to get in touch with the Fellowship of St. Alban and St. Sergius, an informal Anglican-Orthodox ecumenical group, and the House of St. Gregory and St. Macrina in Oxford, an international ecumenical student residence affiliated with the Fellowship. In the garden behind St. Gregory's House is the Orthodox church I first attended.

Early in my first term I saw a notice in my college about an ecumenical student discussion at St. Gregory's House, so I went to it. An Orthodox student gave a talk about how time is transcended in the eucharistic liturgy. I found her approach to be refreshing, fascinating, and compelling, and I eagerly took part in the discussion that followed. Dr. Nicholas Zernov was there, the retired Lecturer in Orthodox Studies at the university and a most extraordinary man. He had a gift for introducing people to Orthodoxy and inviting them to attend the church's services as well as ecumenical gatherings. He could ask personal questions to strangers with such warmth, love, and genuine interest that they were happy to answer and engage in deep conversation, usually about spiritual things. On the third Sunday of each month the Orthodox parish in Oxford would serve the divine liturgy in English, and beforehand Dr. Zernov would give an introductory talk for newcomers. At that first meeting I attended, he invited me to come to the English liturgy as well as to meetings of the Fellowship of St. Alban and St. Sergius, and I went. I was one of many whom he brought to their first liturgy, and one of many who eventually joined the Church into which he introduced them. May his memory be eternal.

At that same first meeting an Orthodox doctoral student in theology named Elizabeth Moberly was also present. I met her briefly and thought nothing of it at the time. But the next day was a Friday, and I went into London on the train to visit my aunt for the weekend. Providentially, Elizabeth happened to be sitting across the compartment from me. She remembered meeting me the night before and struck up a conversation. We talked on the train all the way to London, and she became my closest friend during those two years in Oxford. When I felt depressed, she would invite me to visit her. We talked for hours over cups and cups of tea. She later moved to Philadelphia, where she now lives. She conducts workshops and writes about ethical and psychological issues.

In Oxford I continued to attend ecumenical meetings involving the Orthodox and went to their services from time to time. At first the liturgy was a bit strange, but it included things I knew from the Episcopal services at Yale which I missed in all the other Anglican services. I was impressed with the intense reality and depth of the Orthodox worship as well as its unspeakable beauty. My experience was and still is that it truly makes God's Kingdom present on earth. However, my awareness of this grew slowly over several years, and during that time I found it important to attend both Anglican and Orthodox services.

Throughout my two years in England I went to many Orthodox-inspired lectures and meetings as well as to their church, and I lived at St. Macrina's House over the summer. My biggest problem with the Orthodoxy I knew in that country was that most of the worship was in Greek or Slavonic, and there was little in English, especially then in the middle to late 70's. While there I made a decision never to join the Orthodox Church, and one of the main reasons was that it seemed I would have to convert to Greek or Russian culture as well, and I knew I lacked the ability and the motivation to do this.

Nevertheless, Orthodoxy had become an abiding interest for me, and I liked the Church's theology better than all the other forms of Christian teaching I encountered. Early in my Oxford days I read Archimandrite Kallistos Ware's *The Orthodox Church* and Vladimir Lossky's *Mystical Theology of the Eastern Church* and found them fascinating and compelling. I also met Fr. Kallistos, who was later to become Bishop of Diokleia, and became one of his students. I attended many of his lectures and had him as a tutor, and he became a major influence in my life, more so than I realized at the time. He is an excellent teacher as well as a fine pastor. He has an exceptionally clear and balanced mind and a tremendous gift for explaining Orthodoxy to Western people. It was really he who taught me the Church's faith, although at the time I thought I could believe and practice it as an Episcopalian. Since Anglicanism allowed me to believe almost anything I wanted, my choice was Orthodox theology.

I was also impressed with the way Fr. Kallistos combined monasticism and scholarship, and I wished that somehow I could follow his example in this, though I did not think it was possible and tried to put the whole issue out of my mind. He has proven to be an important role model for me as well as a teacher and pastor.

After Oxford I wanted to do a Ph.D. in theology emphasizing Christian doctrine. Vanderbilt University in Nashville offered me a big scholarship and I knew it had a good academic reputation, so I went there. In England it was difficult to tell what it would really be like. It turned out to be primarily a liberal Protestant island in a sea of conservative Protestant culture, and I was uncomfortable with both. I only found one professor there with whom I shared common interests and had trouble finding a church community I liked. I was involved in the charismatic group described above until I broke with it around March. Although I tried a number of Episcopal congregations, I did not like any of them and found myself primarily attached to the Roman Catholic chaplaincy, as did quite a few other non-Catholic students. This congregation was liturgical and believed the central doctrines of the Christian faith. It also had daily services, which were important to me. I worshipped there regularly, and the chaplains were happy to give me communion since I believed in Christ's real presence in the Eucharist. However, I always knew I could not become a Catholic since I could not accept some of their doctrines. The Pope was a problem to me as was the Filioque. I also needed the freedom to affirm some Orthodox doctrines Rome did not accept like the essence-energies distinction. I think there was a Greek Orthodox church in Nashville then, but I never tried to go to it. I knew the liturgy would probably be in Greek. Besides, I lived on campus without a car. It was remote from my thoughts as well as seeming far away culturally and geographically.

At the end of the spring semester I decided to leave Vanderbilt and go to the Graduate Theological Union at Berkeley the next fall. But before returning to my parents' home in southern California for the summer I went on vacation to the northeastern states. Two of my closest friends from the Episcopal Church at Yale were getting married in Dwight Chapel, and I wanted to be there. The bride arranged for me to stay in New Haven with Barbara Newman, a graduate student who had arrived after I left for England. She also had an interest in Orthodoxy, and we immediately became friends. I also got to know an undergraduate from the Episcopal group named Steve Morris who had become a catechumen at an Orthodox parish in New York City.

My flight home to California departed from Kennedy Airport on a Sunday afternoon, so Steve, Barbara and I together with two other Yale graduate students attached to the Episcopal chaplaincy went to Manhattan for the day. We attended the divine liturgy at Steve's parish, which belonged to the Orthodox Church in America. This was the first Orthodox service I had attended since leaving England almost a year before. It was all in English, and it was glorious. I suddenly realized that *this* was what I had been missing in Nashville. I discovered that in America it is possible to be Orthodox without converting to a foreign language or culture.

After the liturgy, Steve stayed there for a catechetical class. He is now Fr. Stephen Morris, pastor of St. Mary Magdalen Mission in upper Manhattan, which was founded by members of that same parish. The rest of us went on to a service at the Cathedral of St. John the Divine so that we could receive communion. The contrast with the liturgy we had just attended could not have been greater. One of the cathedral's side chapels had been turned into a Shinto shrine. The sermon was a dialogue between the dean and Buckminster Fuller. The famous architect expounded his philosophy in language I found largely unintelligible, but clearly it had nothing to do with Christianity. The dean went on and on about how brilliant and spiritually insightful Fuller was and hoped that one of his sculptures would be installed in the church as a permanent monument to him.

Soon after my return to California I summoned up the courage to visit the Orthodox parish nearest my parents' home, which is St. Innocent Church in Tarzana. It is perhaps the oldest all-English language congregation in the country. I went to many services there that summer, though I attended an Episcopal parish on Sunday mornings and at other times. As I prepared to leave for Berkeley in September, 1978, I asked the priest at St. Innocent to recommend an Orthodox church in that area. He sent me to St. Michael the Archangel Mission in Walnut Creek, which at the time was the English language congregation closest to Berkeley.

However, I had not given up on Anglicanism. In Berkeley I lived in the dorm at the Church Divinity School of the Pacific, the Episcopal seminary belonging to the Graduate Theological Union. As a Ph.D. student, I took classes at other member schools of the Union and at the University of California nearby, but for community purposes I was attached to CDSP. I thought I would find the healthy Anglican ethos there that was lacking in Nashville. To complicate matters further, one of the chaplains who had baptized me had moved to San Francisco and was starting a mission there similar to the Yale chaplaincy group I had loved so much. He had services on Tuesday evenings, and I attended regularly. I became one of the first five official members of the mission, which was dedicated to St. Gregory of Nyssa. I also went to St. Michael Orthodox Mission on Saturday evenings and Sunday mornings and on weekdays to the morning and evening services at the Episcopal seminary. I was happy to have daily liturgical worship again, as I'd had in England. Berkeley reminded me of Oxford a great deal.

Years later I wrote my dissertation on Gregory of Nyssa, and I do not think he would have approved of much of what that San Francisco mission did. The priest had moved on from his interest in Orthodoxy and was experimenting with other things. In the meantime, my perspective had changed during my two years of study with Fr. Kallistos in Oxford. But it took me another academic year to reach my final disillusionment with Episcopalianism, to which I was still very loyal. To arrive at that point, I had to experience disappointment over and over, and that is what happened. At CDSP there were daily sermons by faculty or students, and it seemed that almost every time the preaching contained what I regarded as theological error. There was also liturgical experimentation with which I was not comfortable. This sometimes happened at St. Gregory's Mission as well. It was refreshing to see that at the Orthodox church it never happened.

My priest in San Francisco invited his congregation to engage in discussion following his sermons. One time a woman there said that often she had trouble believing in God's existence. Everyone else in the group admitted to similar doubts, and then the priest responded by saying that some weeks he believed in God one day out of seven and some weeks six days out of seven. Everyone was calm and mutually supportive in this, and I was shocked. I said, "I know that I know that I know that God exists." The group was supportive of my view as well and discussed it further, but I felt like a minority of one. That spring the experimental Holy Thursday service was held during dinner at someone's home, and the priest told us it would be like an early Christian liturgy. A parishioner had baked two round loaves of bread, a small one for the Eucharist and a large one for the meal. The priest decided to use the large one for the Eucharist, and he "consecrated" it by reciting a few words from the *Didache*, a primitive Christian document. Then we all ate chunks of this loaf with our dinner! Nobody else seemed to mind. To make matters worse, the priest then preached a sermon saying that communion, which he equated with Jesus's table fellowship, should be given to everybody, while baptism should be reserved for committed believers. I later learned that he had probably learned this sacramental theology from his bishop, who held the same view and was proud of it.

I left St. Gregory's Mission in May, and by this time I was thoroughly disillusioned with the Episcopal Church. To complicate matters again, at about the same time the couple who had been giving me rides to the Orthodox mission in Walnut Creek had decided to stop taking me. I concluded, wrongly as it happened, that I was no longer welcome there, so I stopped going. I later learned it was only this one rather snobbish couple who had taken a dislike to me. They liked to criticize a lot of things, including what they perceived as "tackiness" in the way the priest served, and I found their attitude inappropriate.

Meanwhile, I was left ecclesiologically adrift. I wondered whether institutionalized religion was the problem, and whether any church could offer me authentic participation in worship without unacceptable strings attached. That summer I attended Roman Catholic services in Berkeley along with some Episcopal ones. There was an Eastern Rite Catholic congregation that I liked, but I still could not see Rome as a viable option. The Roman Catholic understanding of the Papacy and some other doctrines remained unacceptable to me.

At the end of the summer of 1979, while visiting my family in Los Angeles, I again attended services at St. Innocent Orthodox Church and, during a particularly glorious vigil service on the eve of the Feast of the Exaltation of the Cross, I found myself thinking, not for the first time, "This is so beautiful! Why don't I join the Orthodox Church?" But I was still committed to the decision I had made in Oxford never to join. I regarded my "Why not?" as a tempting thought and put it out of my mind.

Afterward, as I walked in the door of my parents' home, the telephone rang. It was my old friend John RePass, calling from St. Vladimir's Seminary in New York. He had discovered Orthodoxy and had gone to study there. "Curiosity finally got to me," he said. "Since you are so knowledgeable about it, why haven't you joined the Orthodox Church?"

As we talked, I realized I had forgotten almost all of the reasons I had once found so convincing. This conversation, whose timing was surely arranged by God's providence, was what finally shook my resolution never to become Orthodox. Shortly after this, I returned to Berkeley for my second year of doctoral study. I was in considerable spiritual turmoil about the Orthodox Church. When I was chrismated a month after that call, on October 14, 1979, John was embarrassed and wondered whether he had pressured me too much. But when a great snow bank on the side of a mountain is poised to slide, a pebble falling in precisely the right spot can set off an avalanche.

Following my baptism I needed to explore all the options in Christianity that appeared viable to me, and having done so I found that all of them had led me to dead ends except one. One of my biggest problems with the Orthodox had always been their claim to be the one true Church. On the basis of my rich and varied experience, it was important to me to be able to affirm the truth and spiritual life I had found in other churches; and the fact that although problems existed, many people I knew in all of them were real Christians graced with genuine faith, prayer, and love for God. I could not write them all off, and I certainly could not deny the validity of my own conversion and baptism. The trouble was that I had reached a point where I had to admit the Orthodox claim was correct after all. I did not have to deny any truth I found elsewhere. I only had to acknowledge that it was partial and in places distorted, which my experience now told me it was, and that the fullness of truth and life in Christ is found in the Orthodox Church.

As I wrestled with these issues, it became clear that I had to join the Orthodox Church. Now that I believed it to be the true Church, remaining outside it was no longer a viable option. In prayer, I perceived that Christ was in the Orthodox Church beckoning me to come to him there. I could not refuse him.

I called Fr. Michael Prokurat, the pastor at St. Michael, and said I wanted to see him about something important. He was actually a fellow doctoral student of mine at the Graduate Theological Union, so from the beginning he viewed me as an academic colleague. In addition, he had always been very sensitive and understanding about the situation of women interested in ministry in the Church. He took this positive attitude for granted since he regarded it as the truth, and it was only later that I learned not all Orthodox priests and lay leaders share it. It was a blessing to me that this man, a scholar and good pastor, was the one who received me into the Church and became my first confessor.

When he met with me I told him in fear and trembling of my decision that I wanted to join the Orthodox Church. Was I motivated by decisions the Episcopalians had recently made regarding women priests? I said no. That had had nothing to do with my decision. Half of the students at the Church Divinity School were women and as many of them had genuine faith and gifts for ministry as the men. I considered them and their vocations worthy of respect. Since the Episcopalians have changed so many other, more important things, why should they not have women in the priesthood, as well? Nor was my decision based on objections to liturgical revisions contained in their new Prayer Book, since I knew that when done well services based on it could be as beautiful as the older kind.

My problem with the Episcopal Church concerned more essential things. It seemed that for them everything had become optional, including the core doctrines of the Christian faith and serious commitment to spiritual life. How could so many of their clergy and laity sing beautiful musical settings of the Nicene Creed without believing what the words said, and, worse still, not see this inconsistency as an issue?

I remember the words of a conservative Anglo-Catholic priest, who was also a professor emeritus of theology, after the Sunday service at a high church parish, that "the doctrine of the Trinity is an outdated 4th century concept." Neither the rector, a man of strong traditional faith, nor anyone else there saw any problem with him. Episcopalians seem to have no qualms about being in communion with others who share little or none of the same faith. Those among them who are still devout Christians must somehow come to terms with this, and I do not know how they do it. It turned out to be something I could no longer accept.

As an Episcopalian, I could believe what I knew to be true, but others would consider it only my opinion and say that it might not be true for someone else. When I became Orthodox, I could say exactly the same things and know that the whole Church was behind me. It made a big difference that I now spoke for the Church as a whole, not only for myself. After my chrismation, I found I could have the same dinner table conversations with students at CDSP as I'd had previously, but they were more willing to listen to my views and treat them with respect, since I now represented another honorable tradition instead of being a theological challenge within their own.

I had fears that because I left their church while living among them they would regard me as a traitor. One night that fall I dreamed that someone had broken into my dorm room and smashed all the icons, and that I was left kneeling there looking at the broken pieces on the floor. But nothing like that ever happened. Instead, people at the Episcopal seminary were more supportive of me at that moment than before or after. When I told them of my decision, they said, "I was wondering when you were going to do that," and, "I know you have been thinking about it for a long time," and, "We're glad you've found something that will make you happy." I had only been thinking about it consciously for a few weeks, but my neighbors knew long before I did and were not surprised.

Such open-mindedness may be the greatest strength of the Anglicans, but it is also their greatest weakness. My five and a half years in their church gave me the space to do the spiritual explorations I needed to do, which was a blessing, but it could not be my permanent home. All along, I had had to supplement Episcopalian worship with other forms of spirituality, including the Orthodox. I was always piecing different things together and never found the wholeness and fullness of faith and life in Christ there. Eventually, my explorations led me to move on to where I have found that fullness.

When I met with Fr. Michael, we had a pleasant, low key conversation. I told him that although I attended the services I felt I was missing something by not receiving the sacraments in the Orthodox Church. At the end he asked whether I had any further questions. "Yes," I said, "How long do I have to wait?" I somehow had the idea that the O.C.A. had a standard policy of making people wait a year once they made the decision to join, and I had been dreading this. The thought of being cut off from the sacraments and not truly belonging to anything for so long was another reason why I had hesitated to take this step, but I was determined to endure this if necessary. Fr. Michael answered that since I had been taught the faith by Fr. Kallistos Ware, which was as good a catechism as he could imagine, and since I had attended St. Michael the Archangel Mission for a year, we could do it as soon as I thought I was ready. At this moment, a great weight rolled off my shoulders, and I was profoundly thankful to Fr. Michael. I returned to his parish, and ten days after that conversation I was chrismated.

I immediately discovered that by not receiving the Orthodox sacraments I had been missing more than I could ever have imagined. At least in my experience, the Orthodox eucharist has proven to be very intensely real and far more effectual than the communion I had received so many times in Anglican and Roman Catholic churches. Within a few months, I had moved far from the Anglican spirituality with which I had been at home for so long. For a while I continued to go to morning and evening services at the Episcopal seminary, not taking communion but using them as a daily office. In time, however, I stopped attending. It got to a point where the theological error and liturgical tinkering made me so uncomfortable I could no longer pray there.

After my chrismation I lived at CDSP for three more academic years. I had begun my doctoral study at the Graduate Theological Union with a specialization in systematic theology, but I soon realized that the faculty in that department were not even asking the same kinds of questions as I. I wanted to learn about the classic issues in Christian doctrine such as the Trinity, Christology, soteriology and so forth. They were asking whether theology is possible and whether it makes sense to speak of God at all. So early in my second year there, having become Orthodox, I realized that I could best approach what I considered the real theological issues by studying patristics. The doctoral program at GTU is a long one for virtually everybody. It took me eight years, which is not unusual, and I completed it in May 1986. Following that I stayed on in Berkeley and did further research and writing on the Fathers.

Chrismation is the beginning of life in the Church, not the end. Since then my life in Christ has continued to grow in depth and richness, as I expect, by God's grace, it always will, unless I turn away from him, a thing I cannot imagine ever wanting to do. What is so wonderful about Orthodoxy is that the life of the Church is infinite and unbounded. The Holy Trinity dwells there together with the Mother of God, the holy angels, and all the saints. Though we, the faithful on earth, are unworthy, they are present with us and invite us into an ever-increasing communion of love with them and with each other. This means that I can always continue onward in my journey toward God *within* the Church. I will never encounter an insurmountable obstacle or a limit to its spiritual resources, as I did in all the other churches, which would require me to leave and go beyond it in order to continue moving toward God.

This is not the place to describe the whole history of my life in the Church since my chrismation, but I do want to say more about two important aspects of it, my involvement in monasticism and my experience as a woman interested in ministry.

For several years before I joined the Church, I went to morning and evening services whenever possible, and usually at least one service a day. For the most part I also went to communion daily. This practice was very important to me. When I became Orthodox, these opportunities were no longer available. At first I found the sacramental and liturgical life so fulfilling that I did not miss the daily worship too much, but within a couple of years I was again longing for it.

Since shortly after my baptism I had an interest in monastic life. I would talk to someone about it on occasion, but generally I put it out of my mind. I feared it would involve greater suffering than I could bear. I also believed I had a moral obligation to do something more productive with my intellectual talents, and I knew I could not tolerate a situation where I would be denied the freedom to use them. Meanwhile, I visited various Anglican, Catholic, and Orthodox communities. Some aspects of their life seemed to me like heaven on earth and other aspects like hell on earth. I could not approach the issue of my relationship to monastic life dispassionately. My feelings about it were too strong, conflicted, and disturbing, so I decided it was something I could not handle, treated it as a tempting thought (like my desire to join the Orthodox Church!), and made great efforts to persuade myself that I wasn't interested. I thought I had succeeded in this, though I never did entirely.

One thing, however, was clear. I have always known, since the beginning of my life as a Christian, that I could not have a relationship with a man without somehow betraying Christ. I acknowledged that marriage is an honorable calling for other people, but for me it would have meant putting someone else in his place, which was and still is unthinkable. I heard recently that today 40% of the adults in this country are single, and most of them are unhappy with their singleness. This surprises me because I never felt that way.

In the fall of 1981, I spoke to Fr. Michael about my interest in monasticism. He said he thought it was a good thing for me to pursue, and he sent me to a small women's community in northern California, one that no longer exists. For five months beginning that December, I was there as a postulant, though I continued my doctoral studies and went back and forth between there and Berkeley. The quiet and the daily worship were wonderful, and I got a lot of studying done. The prayer brought me great joy and at times it felt like heaven on earth, but unfortunately my life there turned into the opposite.

It was not a healthy community. Two people who held responsible positions there were at war with each other, and it got progressively worse. Although I tried to stay out of it, inevitably I was caught in the crossfire as the community fell apart around me, and I had to leave. This was extremely painful, and it took me a year to recover from it.

Once that year had passed I realized I had learned many positive things at the monastery, and ever after I desired to recover the good aspects of the way of life I had there. While there, we often did reader services without a priest, and this was something I wanted to do myself at home, so I could pray a daily office again. It turned out not to be easy. The Byzantine rite is complicated, many parish priests did not know in detail how to do the weekday services, especially Matins, my favorite, and there were few available English translations of texts from the *Octoechos* and the *Menaion* that I would need. I spent years bit by bit acquiring liturgical texts and learning how to use them with help from several people, especially from Mother Susanna at the Skete of the Holy Virgin of Kazan in Santa Rosa, California. This is the community to which I now belong.

In the fall of 1986, after I had finished my doctorate, I found I was troubled by thoughts that I would like to become a nun but continue to live in my own apartment in Berkeley and do scholarly work. I knew that the Church often disapproves of monastics not living in community, so I felt this was a tempting thought, a radical, unworkable idea. But I was unable to put it out of my mind successfully and it became a persistent distraction in my prayer. I brought it to confession, hoping that Fr. Michael would help me overcome the temptation. Instead, to my surprise, he said he thought it was a good idea, and that I should pursue it. We spoke about it several more times, and then we spoke to two other respected priests who have close ties to Mount Athos. I thought they would disapprove, but instead they also supported the idea and said they regarded it as quite traditional. I had been in the diocese for some years by then, and my work and way of life were known to the church community. Bishop Tikhon of San Francisco gave the proposal his blessing and encouragement, though it was not yet clear specifically how I would live it out.

That summer I went for a two month trip and came home exhausted. Upon my return I was plunged into a period of intense spiritual darkness and struggle that lasted for about a year and a half. With help from God, I gradually came out of it, having grown personally and spiritually in important ways. But at the time it was very painful to me that I could find no priest who understood my difficulties, and in confession I always risked being misunderstood and hurt.

Although some of my trouble was personal, in part it was due to my situation as a theologically educated woman in the Church. It would be a mistake to minimize this aspect of it. I had thought that when I got my Ph.D. I would finally be noticed by church leaders, but it didn't happen. I felt that the Church was trying to confine me within a lay parishioner box, and it did not fit. When parishes asked for volunteers, they always needed people to sing, cook, clean, or teach children, or to do similar jobs for which I had no talent. The priests usually did what little adult religious education there was, and although I had tried to get involved several times, it had not worked out. The only "ministry" available to me was church reading, which I did well, but even there I was only a substitute for the male, ordained reader. Then the reading I'd done was taken away from me when I returned from my two month trip. So I felt that I did not have the talents I needed to be a good Orthodox Christian, and that the Church had rejected the talents I did have.

It was all I could do to force myself to go to Sunday liturgy, and a few times I could not even bring myself to do that. But at least, I thought, the question of monasticism was finally resolved. Since I could barely maintain my commitment to be a member of the Church, that clearly meant I was not called to make any further commitment, or so it appeared.

To keep things as easy as possible, I went to the parish nearest my home, St. John the Baptist Church in Berkeley. Before then I had largely avoided it because it is a Russian congregation and the services are mostly in Slavonic. But I had gone to weekday Liturgies there off and on over the years. The priest, Fr. Nikolajs Vieglais, was in his 80's and had trouble with English, but he was a very loving and gentle man, full of prayer and deeply devoted to the church services. He was a sweet grandfatherly figure, and when I went to confession he would usually absolve me without saying anything. At this point, he was exactly the kind of pastor I needed. I became a member of his parish, to which I still belong, and in a few months I was helping him with a lot of the reading, especially at Saturday vigil and on weekdays. It was my job to supply most of the English the parish used, and eventually this work came to be greatly appreciated by everybody there, including some elderly Russians who are at times suspicious of American converts. Fr. Nikolajs and I were united by a common love for the Church's prayer and liturgical life. He fell asleep in the Lord in June 1992. May his memory be eternal.

During my period of spiritual darkness, I even considered leaving the Orthodox Church. By God's providence, as I was slowly emerging into the light, my old teacher, Bishop Kallistos Ware, came to San Francisco twice in 1988 to lecture. He reaffirmed my faith in Orthodoxy, and during a confession I've always remembered as very encouraging, he asked me how long I had been Orthodox. When I told him eight and a half years, he said that people often have difficulty between their fifth and tenth years, but that after that it usually becomes better. This proved to be true in my case as well.

As things slowly improved, I arrived at a firm conviction that I belong to the Church for the sake of my own worship of God, not in order to use my gifts or have them accepted by the community. I had faced all my earlier temptations to leave Orthodoxy, and now my commitment to the Church was stronger than it had ever been. More recently, however, I have been given more and more opportunities for church service. There is still relatively little I can contribute to local parish life, but I have been active in teaching, lecturing, and writing at the deanery, diocesan, national, and international levels.

My interest in monasticism had gradually returned, and I again asked Bishop Tikhon for guidance. When he visited my parish in January 1990, he told me to go to Archimandrite Dimitry, the elder at the Skete of the Holy Virgin of Kazan in Santa Rosa, and ask that he become my spiritual father, give me a rule of prayer, and teach me monastic life. The rule of prayer is something that a spiritual father traditionally gives to a spiritual child, especially in monasticism. This is how the Church's practices come to be applied appropriately in each person's particular situation.

The understanding was that I could stay in Berkeley and would not have to live with the community but be attached to them. At the Skete a few days later, Fr. Dimitry accepted this arrangement, which has proven to be a great blessing to me. A man of few words filled with great humility, warmth, love, wisdom, and inner strength, his spiritual presence is tangible and profound, and his intercessions are very powerful. This continues to be true although he fell asleep in the Lord, a few weeks after Fr. Nikolajs who was almost exactly his contemporary. There are those who say Fr. Dimitry had the gift of prophesy, which may well have been the case, but what is more important is that he was a very holy man. It has been a blessing to me to have him as my spiritual father and to know that I will always be supported by his prayers. May his memory be eternal.

I was attached to the community, kept the rule of prayer he gave me, and followed his instructions for almost two years before the stroke that left him unable to speak in December 1991. The community clothed me as a novice in March 1992, on the Saturday before Great Lent, when the Church commemorates all monks and nuns throughout history. The sisters warned me that after my clothing I might be faced with severe spiritual warfare, but this did not happen. By God's mercy, these struggles, which were intense and protracted, occurred during the three months just before I was made a novice. As soon as I put on the habit, they disappeared. I think perhaps I had been undergoing the intense inner struggles usually associated with monastic life all along but without adequate resources for handling them. Fr. Dimitry, the community, the rule of prayer, the consistent discipline, and the habit have provided me with much of the spiritual support I lacked in the past, and so more and more I have been blessed with peace, stability, and joy. Trials and temptations continue to occur, but they do not overwhelm me as much as they once did. I acknowledge that my experience is still very small and I could encounter severe struggles in the future, but I am deeply thankful to God for these blessings. I have not yet been tonsured, that is, the Church has not yet given me an official blessing to make a permanent commitment to monastic life. Yet I am convinced, as a wise priest once told me, that all of monastic practice is somehow sacramental. I hope and pray that our Lord will enable me to continue with it always. Moreover, Fr.

Dimitry told me that I will be tonsured in the future, and I believe he was speaking the truth.

I would like to conclude by discussing one further issue that has proven to be central to my experience as a Christian and a monastic. Although Fr. Dimitry told me that I should always consider things he said as spiritual advice and not as obediences, I chose to accept the rule of prayer and several other instructions he gave me as obediences. I think he was pleased with this, and it certainly has been a blessing to me in ways I did not expect. He taught me not in words but by his love, example, and prayers the importance of obedience in monastic life. Some of the blessings it has brought me are difficult to explain and involve deeper participation in the communion among persons that constitutes the life of the Church. Others are clear and practical. It is often immensely helpful to have someone else, the person one is obeying, share the responsibility before God's judgment for difficult decisions one must make. When left to myself I frequently felt I faced moral dilemmas where I was totally accountable to our Lord for making the right choice yet unable to be certain what his will was. My monastic commitment frees me from much of this burden. I have people to consult, whose advice, often common sense and in agreement with what I had thought best anyway, provides me with a second opinion. In addition, following the rule of prayer daily means that at the worst moments of struggle I cannot stray too far from prayer and encounter with God.

My profound fear of obedience was a major reason why I backed so slowly toward monastic life. I believe part of this fear was rooted in American culture. Our country's political system is based on shared responsibility among different levels and branches of government as well as the accountability of elected officials to those they govern. It was established this way so as to guard against anybody exercising absolute power, in the belief that such power when left unchecked could be used to abuse those subject to it. In a fallen world, it is wise to have these safeguards in civic institutions. Today many nations of the former Eastern block are seeking to emulate the Western democracies in this, and I believe it can serve as an appropriate expression of the combined mutual inter-dependence, conciliarity, and hierarchy that Orthodox Christians affirm as intrinsic to human community. However, there is a danger that when we focus on how authority can be misused, we forget how it can be used well.

We also tend to imagine that obedience is an all or nothing matter and is only given to totalitarian dictators. In actuality, all of us practice obedience in everyday situations. We give it to family members, teachers, employers, or police officers. It generally pertains to limited and specific activities, and in cases of difficulty is often open to negotiation. The same thing happens in monastic life. If I am told to do something and it isn't working, it is generally appropriate to go back to the person who gave the instruction, explain the reason for my difficulty, and ask what to do about it. If that person has good will and common sense, which he or she usually has, we can then discuss it and resolve the problem. In cases of long standing, serious, and unresolved difficulties, monastics can ask for a blessing to look for another spiritual father or another community. In practice, unless there is a situation of severe abuse, this permission is usually granted when there is a good reason for it. As I learned these things, my fear of being imprisoned for life in intolerable conditions by my commitment to obedience was greatly relieved.

However, my fear had roots in my early life as well as in American cultural attitudes. As a child I really wanted to obey, but my efforts were repeatedly frustrated. Adults would often tell me to do things that were impossible for me and then punish me for not doing them. At other times, they would tell me to do one thing and when I did it insist they had wanted something else, so again I was punished. My own feelings, needs, and experiences were not heard or believed by them. What this taught me was that the situation of owing obedience primarily exposed me to abuse, and the only way to escape the abuse and have space to be myself was to grow up and never have to obey anyone again.

So I spent much of my adult life consciously striving to avoid obligations to obey, while at the same time, unconsciously, retaining the unfulfilled longing to obey that was frustrated in childhood. Without knowing it, I tried too hard to obey everybody, which left me burdened with guilt and confusion in the face of people's often unclear, impossible, or conflicting expectations. To my surprise, the monastic obedience from which I sought so long to protect myself turned out to provide structure I always needed and wanted. Finally, thanks to God, I am receiving the patient guidance I missed as a child in learning how to become good and to do good, but in a context of adult responsibility and common sense. Yet at the core of my being I am still that little girl longing for goodness, truth, and love, for our Lord Jesus Christ who is all these things, and longing to give my life to him in adoration and obedient service. At the heart of the Church's life, through my many sins and mistakes, a little at a time, I am finding my heart's desire.

Glory to God for the blessings he has given me throughout my life, though I am unworthy of them. I have done nothing special to bring about the good things described in this essay. I do not know why God gave me faith when many others do not have it, and I do not know why not everybody has received faith as I have. I can only stand in awe of the mystery and give thanks to God for his gratuitous gifts, praying that all people may receive them. Glory to God in all things. Glory to him forever.

Memoirs of an Unsuccessful Mystic

Barbara Newman

O Lord, send Sophia from thy holy heavens,
and send her down from the throne of thy majesty
that she may be with me and toil with me,
that I may know what is pleasing in thy sight.

Wisdom of Solomon 9:10

It has always been a question of God, and it still is. My tale is the tale of God's ways with one recalcitrant sinner. I do not know how it will end. I do know that, if a Jewish feminist intellectual can find a home in the Orthodox Church, then no one is exempt, no one excluded.

At the age of seven I was taught that Christians went to church and Jews to the synagogue. But not all Jews -- for some, like our family, were enlightened folks who believed in reason, not indoctrination. Or so my father always said, remembering the bitter anti-Semitic taunts of his youth. But the fair dream of reason and tolerance paled for me when my little Catholic friends began to prepare for their first communion. Frothy white dresses hung on the line to dry, and the bric-a-brac of devotion lay strewn about their rooms -- here a set of rosary beads, there a Sacred Heart statue with its mysterious flames and simpering eyes. I asked Lydia what "communion" meant and she couldn't find the right words, but she showed me a holy card. I asked Janet, and she taught me the first sentence of her catechism: "God is the supreme being, infinite in all perfections, who alone exists in himself." Then why, I wondered, did he seem not to exist for me? For "the chief end of man is to glorify God and enjoy him forever."

When I was eleven I stole a Gideon Bible from a motel room and kept it for years, my guilty secret, to be greedily paged by lamplight under the covers. Knowing no better method, I started with Genesis and read straight through to Revelation. What did I learn there? The Preacher's words pierced me with intimations of mortality: "Or ever the silver cord be snapped, or the golden bowl be broken . . . and the dust return unto dust as it was, and the spirit unto God who gave it." Child though I was, I yearned over the Song of Songs: "Stay me with flagons, comfort me with apples; for I am sick of love." When I came to the Lord's Prayer I resolved to say it every night for a year, on the assumption that if God existed he would grant me faith. But the year passed and my agnosticism remained intact, so I gave up prayer as a child might give up chocolate for Lent.

I was fifteen and in love -- desperately, silently, as only a bookish girl with glasses and braces can be. My adored one invited me to his church for Easter, saying the Bach chorales would be so joyful, the stained glass so lovely when it caught fire from the rising sun. And so it was. But while the faithful sang hymns I stood mute, and when it came time to recite the Creed, I conjugated French verbs for Monday's quiz. No lightning struck, no earthquake rocked the foundations of my soul. For years I returned to that church every Easter, hoping for a dramatic conversion like the ones I had read about in William James; but I knew it would never happen.

At nineteen, an angst-ridden college sophomore, I enrolled in every religion class that Oberlin had to offer. I read Kierkegaard's *Fear and Trembling* and *The Sickness unto Death*, and like the squeamish medical student, discovered in myself all the symptoms. I read Barth on predestination and concluded that, if the "non-elect" somehow lacked real existence, then at least God and I had something in common. I read the story of C. S. Lewis's conversion, how he had been dragged "kicking and screaming" into the flock of Christ, as I listened with growing dread to the persuasions of my evangelical roommate, Kitty. Why was it that the knowledge of God I had longed for as a child now loomed as a terrifying threat?

Despairing of a direct approach to my problem, I tried oblique ones. Literature was no refuge from the possible God, I discovered, and neither was love. Transcendental Meditation only bored me. Perhaps music would provide an escape? One January term I spent six hours a day at the piano, railing at my non-existent God for giving me no musical talent -- yet I heard his voice in every note of the *Well-Tempered Clavier*. I enrolled in an Experimental College class called "Celebration and Festivity" (for this was Oberlin, and it was 1972) -- only to find that it was run by a bearded priest and a liturgical dancer. So I studied liturgical dance, and after the performance the director told us to keep the plain wooden crosses we had used as props. All that winter the cross glowered at me from my bedroom wall. I read the *Showings* of Julian of Norwich and fancied it would start to bleed, but had no such vision.

As time went by the pressure grew too heavy to bear. One memorable evening I chanced to overhear my housemates descanting -- in my absence, they thought -- on the catalogue of my thoughtless, self-absorbed, discourteous ways. Suddenly I knew what Scripture meant by the conviction of sin, for was not I myself a lost soul? Claudia, Toni, wherever you are, forgive me! I never had the courage to confess I'd been eavesdropping, much less apologize for my evil deeds. But in grim compunction I sought out my "Festivity" priest, asking if I should be baptized. My greatest fear at this time was that I would apostasize a week later and be more profoundly damned than before. With a wisdom that sounded to my young soul like a counsel of despair, he said only that it would be sad indeed if I still held the same beliefs at forty that I had at twenty. Certainty was what I demanded, and that above all, God wished to deny.

So on that dismal March afternoon, as I trudged across a parking lot and scowled at the remnants of late snow, I knew the time had come to resolve my dilemma. Either God existed -- but I couldn't prove it beyond the shadow of a doubt, and how ludicrous it would be to make such a gross mistake after such long deliberation! Anyhow, if he *did* exist, the ethical demands -- why, the thing was unthinkable! Well then: God clearly did *not* exist, and I had only to forget about him and get on with my life. But in that instant, as the gray Midwestern sky bore down on the graying snow and leached all color from the earth, I saw with horror that I had no life to get on with.

Mercifully that taste of perdition did not last. For my benumbed mind had finally drawn the conclusion that, if God had beaten me in fair fight, then he *must* exist and I had better acknowledge the fact. Retracing my steps, I left a note for Kitty, saying I had been "compelled to come in" and asking what I was supposed to do next? Witness, I suppose: so I wandered off to the dime store on Main Street, bought a cheap crucifix, and hung it around my neck. Then I knelt down in my favorite woodland glade to attempt communion with Nature and Nature's God. Prayer has never come easily to me, and in that hour I perceived only the usual void; but no matter. Four days later, on Holy Saturday, I received baptism at Kitty's church. She stood godmother, triumphant, joyful, while like a sleepwalker I fumbled through the ritual, reciting the Apostles' Creed as though it were a strange and beautiful poem from the planet Tral-famadore. The priest had dispensed with religious instruction because there was so little time. Only later did I learn that his congregation had been praying all through Lent for a catechumen to baptize at the Easter Vigil.

In those first, heady days of my conversion I was only dimly aware that there existed "churches" in addition to "the Church." The one I attended was in fact Episcopalian. After communion every Sunday I would gaze in wonder at my new siblings in Christ and lose myself in exalted dreams of their sanctity. It was, at any rate, easier than cultivating my own. But this idyll was shattered a year later, when I returned from a semester in London to find my beloved parish on the brink of schism. Our priest, Rev. Peter Beebe, was among those prophetic spirits who supported the ordination of women before the Episcopal Church formally allowed it, and he had invited Carter Heyward (one of the famous Philadelphia Eleven) for regular eucharistic celebrations. There followed a "godly admonition" to desist from the bishop, an angry gesture of defiance, and a full-scale ecclesiastical trial, which ended with the pastor defrocked and the parish bitterly divided. My own part in these great doings was nil, but I had been exposed for the first time to an issue that would not, then or ever, go away.

For the time being, it was I who went -- from college straight to divinity school. The University of Chicago was and is a fine institution, but for me, the choice was a poor one. What I sought was community in faith and a degree in medieval theology; what I found was a curriculum steeped in German Protestant thought, an atheist professor of New Testament, and an exquisite Gothic chapel used but twice a year. Nor did I find it easy to be the only person in Swift Hall with neither pipe nor beard, for female seminarians in those days were seen little and heard less. My Christology seminar met on Wednesday afternoons from two to five, and I soon learned to make proper use of the time. I would spend the first hour trying to decipher the professor's jargon; the second, formulating objections and couching them in the neutral guise of a question; and the third, recovering from the master's sardonic reply. Then I would cross the street for my weekly appointment at the university hospital, where I was being treated for an ulcer.

Since the streets of Hyde Park were so unsafe, I used to indulge my passion for long, calming walks by trekking a mile or two each night through the library stacks. One evening when my nervous energy had run out at last, I paused in an unfamiliar annex and found myself holding a French book of theology, translated from the Russian. It turned out to be *Le Verbe incarné* by Sergei Bulgakov -- a book about Sophia, the Wisdom of God, whom my Christology professor had never mentioned. Eighty pages later, I shook my head in a daze and wandered home. Opening my Bible to the *Wisdom of Solomon*, I found there the passage that had inspired Bulgakov and now astonished me: "In her is a spirit intelligent, holy, unique, manifold, subtle . . . . She is a reflection of the everlasting light, an immaculate mirror of the energy of God and image of his goodness. Although she is one, she can do all; in herself unchanging, she makes all things new."

Who was this mysterious "she" and why had I not met her before? I remembered then that in Byzantium there had been a temple dedicated to Hagia Sophia, the Holy Wisdom of God. So the following quarter, bored with Bultmann and Troeltsch, I studied nothing but Byzantine history, immersing myself heart and soul in that glittering, decadent, passionate realm. Until that year I had had little patience with "official" history, the tedious chronicle of politics and wars, but now I found myself memorizing the dates of battles, decrees of "God-loving emperors," even protocols from Constantine Porphyrogenitus's *Book of Ceremonies* -- all for the sake of Sophia. Meanwhile I continued to read Russian theology on the sly, discovering Vladimir Soloviev, Pavel Florensky, Nikolai Berdyaev. That summer I emptied my meager savings account and booked a charter flight to Constantinople, mindful of Yeats's lines: "And therefore I have sailed the seas and come/ To the holy city of Byzantium."

A pilgrimage may be many things, but as another poet has written, its meaning is never what we thought we came for. When I stepped off the plane on a sultry August morning, I was twenty-three and alone. Scornful as always of my elders' wisdom, I had taken little thought for the contemporary land I was visiting, the Muslim land called "Turkey," for I expected to walk straight into the Byzantium of Photius and the Empress Irene. The only map in my possession was a copy of one drawn in the eleventh century, and my suitcase was packed with the little nothings I had been warned I mustn't wear. When I found that I could not walk five minutes without an escort, I thought the aggressive young Turks only a minor nuisance and felt secretly flattered. Still in anguish after breaking up with my college sweetheart, I was outwardly determined to remain celibate for life, yet inwardly grateful for even the crudest male attentions. It was in this frame of mind that I first set foot in Hagia Sophia -- after taking tea with one especially persistent suitor and promising to meet him for dinner on Saturday night.

To my disappointment, the Great Church at first sight bore not the least resemblance to my romantic dreams. Despite the hours I had sighed over art historians' rhapsodies, I beheld the ancient house of God without comeliness or beauty -- despoiled of its glinting mosaics, its frescoes whitewashed, its interior marred by stunningly ill-matched Arabic plaques, its holiness ravaged first by conquest, then by forced secularization. Crossing myself surreptitiously, I was warned by a guard that such gestures were out of place in a museum. Nevertheless I returned day after day, hoping like Soloviev for a vision of Sophia, still sure in my arrogance that I was meant to be a mystic if only God would co-operate. But I had another motive, too, for I was now stirred by historical empathy. So I found myself praying -- with little concrete sense of what I meant -- that I might somehow participate in the destiny of Byzantium.

Saturday night arrived, and like a coward I tried at the last minute to jilt my Turkish date. But we met all the same and charmed away the hours, eating and drinking, dancing, drinking . . . . In 1976 the term "date rape" did not exist, and if it had, I doubt that it would have shed much light on the intentions of a Turkish *flâneur* with a mini-skirted American blonde. Mother of God, have pity! All that followed is a blur: I remember the taste of *raki*, bouts of agonizing sickness, a maze of crooked lanes in the hour before dawn, the pungent scent of hashish mingled with spices and rotting fruit. On the final day of my sojourn I decided to visit Hagia Sophia once more, but first I sought a moment's peace in the cool, tiled serenity of the Blue Mosque, surely the world's loveliest interior. As I strolled barefoot among the Muslims prostrate for midday prayer, I heard someone suddenly call my name -- and there he was, my rapist, with his blithe insouciant grin. The devout were not edified to see him chase me merrily around the shrine, brandishing a trophy of his conquest, while I searched for decades for the mat where my sandals lay.

Fury, shame, sorrow, remorse -- these were not my feelings when I emerged at last and sank onto a bench in the gardens of Hagia Sophia. In a numbness beyond all feeling, I simply waited. I knew I was defiled, unworthy to approach the sacred doors, but I was no longer able to care. Three minutes passed, or perhaps three hours. I gazed at the fabled dome and waited, not for a vision, not for a voice. Perhaps I would sit there until I died; it seemed to make little difference, for there was nowhere to go. Presently I tried to open my eyes. Then I realized they were already open, for I saw the vivid sky, the sun, the dome, the flowers; but I did not see the One who was there. I tried to listen, but there was nothing to hear. Not then, but later, I did remember one word: *kenosis*. My professor at Chicago had defined it as "the last gasp of the attempt to do Christology from above." I defined it, years afterward, as the peace of Her who emptied herself, taking the form of a servant, being found in the likeness of women.

The odd thing about theophanies is that they change everything, yet settle nothing. For the next ten years I struggled to attach a definitive content to that elusive meeting. Did it mean I should enter a convent? join the Orthodox Church? become a Byzantinist? What was the promise contained in that hour: what was given, what was asked? Floundering for an answer, I could only do what I had always done -- pursue my studies, this time as a medievalist at Yale. Happily ensconced in my new life there, I found myself once again part of a church that embodied all I had been seeking and more.

For a few golden years in the mid-70s, the Episcopal Church at Yale -- its very name promising a bastion of upper-class mediocrity -- seemed to me the ikon of God's Kingdom on earth. Few in the congregation were actually Episcopalians, but we were drawn together by a strange and wonderful liturgy that two maverick priests had devised for us, grafting the best of Roman and Anglican chant onto the Liturgy of St. John Chrysostom. With solemn joy, with chaste exuberance we kept the feasts, praying, learning, disputing together in love. Soon, of course, the golden years came to an end: our charismatic fathers moved on and were replaced by a "real" Episcopal priest, who not unnaturally reintroduced the *Book of Common Prayer* and put an end to our Anglo-Byzantine excess. It was only then that some of us turned eastward in earnest. Five of our little band would eventually become Orthodox as we sought to reclaim the treasures we had lost. One of these is now a priest, another a nun.

But my first reaction, on being exposed to the Orthodox liturgy in its unmitigated form, was to consider it worship fit for angels, not humans. How could anyone stand *still* for so long, I wondered? Sybarite that I was and am, I marveled at Orthodox fasting customs, at the lengthy services and penitential prayers. Despite my love for Byzantium, Greek ethnocentrism proved an impregnable barrier. Yet after several months at an energetic OCA parish in New York and a breath of fresh, wholesome air from the monks of New Skete, I became convinced that there was indeed such a thing as American Orthodoxy. *Pascha, kulich,* and *pierogi* could wait, and I didn't need to speak Russian to venerate ikons. At last I presented myself as a catechumen on the Feast of the Transfiguration, 1979, exactly three years after my visit to the holy city. But the road was still full of unexpected turnings, for God never runs out of surprises.

A month later, I was scheduled to return to London, where I had planned to join my new fiancé as we both researched our dissertations at the British Library. This engagement, through God's overwhelming mercy, came to a speedy end before I crossed the sea, but it was too late to change my plans even though, for ecclesiastical as well as academic reasons, it now seemed wiser to stay in New Haven. When I arrived in London anyhow, I knew not a soul in the city except for my ex-boyfriend, and my occupation of solitary research offered few chances to meet people. As an Orthodox catechumen I had, of course, been told that I could no longer receive communion in the Anglican church. Accustomed as I was to the daily eucharist, I began to experience withdrawal pangs like an addict deprived of her fix. God seemed infinitely remote, and human companionship even more so. For several months I searched in vain for a parish where I might continue to receive instruction, but heard only Greek here, Romanian there, Serbian at a third church. For a time I took refuge at Westminster Cathedral simply to hear the Latin, a language I knew and loved.

Among all the churches I visited, I felt especially ill at ease in the Russian cathedral in Ennismore Gardens. Although the priests I met elsewhere all said that was where I belonged, it seemed that the parishioners could talk of nothing but the saintliness of their bishop, Metropolitan Anthony of Sourozh, who was traveling in Russia at the time. "Aha," I brooded, "this must be some bizarre personality cult," thinking of the gurus and swamis who used to attract proselytes in my college days. A firm believer in the adage that power corrupts, I expected little good from bishops and even less from archbishops and metropolitans, whatever *they* were. Having exhausted my options, however, I decided to stay. Looking for such crumbs of instruction as I could glean beneath the master's table, I noticed what seemed like an unlikely source: the City of Westminster's adult education program was offering a night school course entitled

"What is the Russian Orthodox Church?" So, plunking down the modest sum of three pounds, I signed up and betook myself one night to a plebeian district in Kensington, where, seated behind a third-grader's desk at the Mary Boon School, the last thing I expected was another epiphany.

To my chagrin, the instructor turned out to be none other than Metropolitan Anthony (Bloom), now returned from abroad. An old but still shockingly forceful man, he looked the very image of a Russian monk -- black cassock, gray beard -- with the eyes of Christ the tiger burning bright. He spoke that evening about St. Seraphim and what it meant to suffer with God; but he spoke as one listening, and listened as Lake Baikal might listen to the snow. When he accosted me during the tea break, asking who I was and where I was from, I looked at the floor and stammered, "Could you ask me an easier question, please?" Orals at Yale hadn't been half so daunting. As soon as the class was over I ran as if from a thousand devils, not stopping until I was seated on the tube, filled with abject terror yet certain, at the same time, that now I was safe until death and after.

Human love, friendship, generosity had graced my life in abundance. I had been blessed to witness acts of high courage, to hear lectures and sermons of great brilliance. I had met the Beloved in the beauty of his temple, in the calm of luminous prayer, in the icy spaces of affliction. But never before had I seen the face of Christ in his living servant. I understood now why everyone wants to know a saint but nobody wants to live with one, for "the glory of God is a man fully alive." Bishop Anthony loved to quote those words of St. Irenaeus, so disarmingly simple, so true. Over the next eight months I watched as the Gospel, in all its horror and wonder, took flesh for me in the simplest incidents of parish life, the most ordinary conversational gambits. All turned to parable, all became truth enacted.

For that year only, I was given the eyes of a disciple, observing as the desert novices must have observed their *abba*, constantly discouraged yet constantly starting anew, riding out storms of despair and hope in the face of a supernatural calm. That winter, as it happened, the Gurdjieff-inspired film *Meetings with Remarkable Men* was drawing large crowds in London. I avoided it like the plague; one such meeting was enough! The "personality cult" still unnerved me, all the more as I realized I was in danger of joining it. But as the liturgical year slipped by -- Advent and

Christmas, Theophany, Great Lent, Holy Week and Pascha -- the timeless "today" of each troparion became a statement of present fact. Once, as I bent to kiss the cross after liturgy, I looked up to smile and mutter a greeting that died on my lips, for there gazing down on me were the eyes of the Crucified: eyes filled with the immensity of pain, and beyond the pain unspeakable joy, and beyond the joy a challenge, as if to say, "You will? Come on then, I dare you!"

In the fullness of time I took up that dare, uttering the vows I have so often betrayed before and since: the vow of martyrdom and the vow of cheerfulness until my dying breath. As I received the holy chrism I half believed that a firing squad stood at attention outside the church, waiting to test the truth of my word. The next day I attended a prayer vigil for Christians in the Soviet Union, who were suffering intense persecution at that time, and the solidarity I had sworn with such heroes made me wonder if I were a hypocrite or just plain mad. As I had done seven years before, after my baptism, I imagined myself the sole unworthy member of so brave a fellowship. This time, however, I was determined to become worthy. I would abandon my dissertation on St. Hildegard, as yet unwritten. I would renounce my few worldly goods, return to America, and find some menial job to pay off my graduate loans; and then I would take the veil at New Skete and embrace the only life worth living. Though I well knew that the nuns of New Skete don't actually wear veils, I was still a medievalist at heart -- and still more a romantic.

My parents would be horrified, of course, but they had weathered my conversion and, in time, they would weather this blow as well. Fortunately for them, Bishop Anthony turned out to possess common sense among his other virtues. He must have seen at once that I was no contemplative. What he said, however, was that since I had already accepted substantial funds to complete my degree, I owed it to myself and my benefactors to do so: it was well to keep the commitments one had made in good faith. Afterward, if I still wished to try the monastic way, I might ask for his blessing. Only years later did I realize that the respect he professed for scholarship, which I took for irony at the time, was quite simple and genuine. In the meantime, I returned to Yale, wrote the dissertation, and became what my talents and training had prepared me to be all along -- an academic.

Though I continued even as a young professor to cherish monastic dreams, at length I perceived a humbling truth. All my life I had sought out "remarkable men" and women, people whose spirituality I idealized and tried to appropriate, in the fond belief that I could absorb grace by osmosis and achieve sanctity by association. Awed by the ascetic path of Bishop Anthony, I wished to claim it for my own, rejecting the very different gifts I had received and the vocation they required. But as soon as I was left to my own resources, and those of a quite ordinary middle-class parish, I discovered that try as I might, I could no longer spend hours every day in prayer, and God showed no more sign of calling me to the mystical life than he ever had. But mere disillusionment was not enough. I had to fall from an even dizzier height into a deeper abyss before I could understand.

It was Sophia who had first lured me to the Orthodox fold, and Sophia whom I continued to love and long for. From my theological and biblical studies, I knew that the same One who is manifest as Sophia in the Old Testament appears to us as Christ in the New. The Scriptures reveal the second Person of the Trinity in both feminine and masculine guise, a mysterious sign to teach us that God is beyond gender and yet humans, female and male, are equally made in God's image. From my patron saints, Hildegard of Bingen and Julian of Norwich, I had learned that "as truly as God is our Father, so truly is God also our Mother." But now, as I gained a richer knowledge of the Western mystics, I mourned that Sophia seemed so little evident in contemporary Orthodox life, the Great Church of Byzantium notwithstanding. With this recognition came a new spiritual and emotional need. Just as I had encountered Christ in the person of Bishop Anthony, I wished now to meet Sophia in a living woman. Since I had been blessed with a spiritual father, I reasoned, would God deny me a spiritual mother as well? How else could the regeneration of my soul be complete?

But in Bishop Anthony I had met someone rare indeed: a man humble enough to deflect idolatrous devotion and faithful enough to remain in Christ's shadow, stepping aside like the Baptist because the light was God's, not his own. This time I was not so fortunate. Fixing my gaze on a close friend, I tried once more to play the disciple's role, to absorb the spiritual gifts and achievements of another woman instead of developing my own. In imagination I cast myself in the role of handmaid and fantasized, drunk with the spirit's greed, that I had become a martyr of sacrificial love. In fact, however, I had fallen headlong into what the ascetic fathers call *prelest,* or spiritual delusion. As I sought to humble myself in the name of selfless devotion, I not only gave way to every masochistic impulse in the depths of my psyche, but led my friend into grave temptation. For she could not resist the deadly gift of my idolatry, and we embarked on a mutually destructive course that ended only with a painful rift and a serious psychological crisis for us both.

But the hardest lessons are the most deeply learned in the end. In this encounter, as in my pilgrimage to Hagia Sophia, I failed to attain what I thought I wanted. I never saw the light of Mount Tabor, never heard angels sing; I never welcomed the mystic Spouse into the bridal chamber of my soul. Instead I learned a truth so plain it is almost banal, but I learned it in my bones: self-giving is not the same as self-destruction. The impulse that masquerades as selfless love may be no more than the sin of envy, and Christian humility -- which I had taken for the opposite of self-acceptance -- is nothing but its baptized cousin. My illumination this time came from an unexpected source: nine months of therapy with a woman who taught me, week after excruciating week, to look honestly at what I meant by "love" and why I despised the flawed, but not altogether futile, self that God meant to redeem. In the process, I came to appreciate more deeply the wisdom of feminist thought, which is indeed one of the Spirit's gracious gifts to our age. As psychologists like Ann Ulanov and Carol Gilligan have seen, it is no wonder that women find it difficult to achieve a mature, centered identity, for our culture has taught us from girlhood to confuse altruism with masochism. Jesus told us to love our neighbors as ourselves; but if we cannot know and value the image of God in ourselves, what wholesome gifts can we give our neighbor? Through my struggle for self-acceptance, I found an unsuspected freedom beyond idolatry -- and the joy of marriage to a man I could finally love without martyrdom and admire without adoration: "Hear, O Israel: the Lord your God is one God; him alone shall ye worship."

But what would become of my quest for Sophia? Like the question of women priests, which cast its lights and shades over my earliest experience as a Christian, the question of Sophia will not disappear from my horizon. I remain more convinced than ever that, just as each of us must struggle against our private idolatries, all of us together must fight the idolatries that bedevil our common life. And one of these (though few will agree with me) is what feminists called Patriarchy: the idolatry of the masculine gender. We claim to believe that our God is bodiless and sexless, that "begetting" is only a metaphor, that men and women alike are formed in God's image. But if we really mean what we say, why do we continue to use only the pronouns "He" and "His" and to exclude half of the people of God from the ministry of Christ? Why do we praise the Father and the Son while ignoring the Scriptural witness to God our Mother, Holy Wisdom, She Who Is? Beyond the vagaries of my idiosyncratic search, I am certain that the full meaning of Sophia for the Orthodox Church has yet to be discovered.

Needless to say, such views have won little sympathy in Orthodox circles. To my astonishment and joy, however, in the summer of 1989 I received a small packet from a dear friend in London. It proved to be a set of taped lectures recently delivered by Bishop Anthony on the subject of men and women in the Church. These profound and difficult talks have not yet been published, but in them the bishop observes that "if you take the situation of women in the Church, it is a debased situation, a situation of enslavement, a situation in which woman is overpowered by a hierarchical system made and exercised by men." This state of affairs does not arise out of God's will or Christ's command, but quite simply out of human sin, the all-too-familiar exploitation of the weak by the strong. In the beginning, God did not make Adam first to be master and Eve second to be the slave. Rather, Adam -- according to an ancient speculation of the Fathers -- "was created as a total human being containing all that is man and all that is woman, all masculinity, all femininity." If we understand the original Adam in this way, then it is clear that the female was not created "from" the male as a secondary and derivative being. Rather, woman and man together were differentiated from a unique, androgynous wholeness, in order to experience the mystery of otherness and mutual love. Christ, the new Adam and the fulfillment of the human race, is no less whole and perfect than the first Adam, "containing within himself all that is man and all that is woman, all masculinity, all femininity." This indeed is one reason the Scriptures represented him in the person of Sophia.

Such a perception of Christ also has significant consequences for our salvation, as Bishop Anthony goes on to assert. St. Athanasius argued against the heretics long ago that "'What Christ has not taken upon himself he has not saved.' If he is nothing but a male he has saved the male half of humanity and the female half is out of salvation or can be dragged into it by some sort of theological trick, but not organically, really." But this is of course unthinkable, for the Church has always affirmed the equality of the sexes in baptism and in the whole life of sanctification. We must recognize, then, that "Christ contained himself the fullness of what is man *and* woman": the divine Word assumed the whole of our humanity. In consequence, "If we speak of him as the High Priest of creation, we must by the same token recognize that in him all . . . the world of woman participates in this sacred function, the priesthood of all creation."

I am told that even Bishop Anthony's devoted London flock has greeted statements like these with consternation and dismay. Only half in jest, he has challenged the powers that be to burn him as a heretic. But as for me, when I read such words and look back on my own variegated journey, I feel that I have come full circle. Despite my youthful longings, my path has been utterly different from his, and incomparably less exalted. But the same conclusions he has arrived at through decades of prayer, ascetic practice, and pastoral labor -- and through his deep familiarity with the mind of the Fathers -- I have reached by another route. God has called me to be not a contemplative nun, but a feminist scholar and teacher, and my way Godward has led through the sorrowful as well as the joyful mysteries, through the God-forsakenness of rape as well as the luminosity of friendship, love, and learning. But all along the way the Lord Jesus has been my light, and the gracious Sophia, and the scintillating Spirit.

In the small world of academe where I live and work, Christians of any kind are rare, and Orthodox Christians virtually nonexistent. To profess oneself a believer is quaint -- an eccentric stance that may provoke any response from mild contempt to benign amusement. Conversely, to declare oneself a feminist in the Orthodox Church is to risk either disbelief or fury. A left-leaning Jewish intellectual with a Catholic husband, feminist or not, is hardly your typical convert. For the past decade, therefore, I have lived with a kind of spiritual schizophrenia, for I have grown up bilingual in two cultures that are scarcely on speaking terms. But paradox, the coinherence of opposites, should be nothing new to an Orthodox Christian. In the homeless child we are trained to recognize the eternal God; in the virgin, the mother; in *kenosis*, the plenitude of life. Why not, then, an Orthodox feminism and a feminist Orthodoxy? If this be heresy, here I must stand. Yet I think it no heresy, but Sophia's truth.

Through a Glass Brightly

By Margaret Long

Metanoia for me was such a total experience of change that afterwards I was not the same person. Something indelible happened. It was like Alice walking through the Looking Glass where everything is reversed. Priorities and perspective shifted and the alarming thing was that I expected everyone else to think as I did. They didn't, and the landscape was often fairly peopleless.

To find and convert to Orthodoxy in middle years was not something I did lightly. Probably my life had been moving towards it. The sorrows, the joys, the follies, the losses, the learning, the longing, and the unanswered questions were all part of the journey. Afterwards I could not delete myself much as I'd have liked to. I am sure that God has reasons for allowing our uniqueness, but the darkness has to be used, like the humus in which a seed is broken.

Since the pattern of a broken jigsaw puzzle is only complete at the end when you see the whole of it, perhaps I should start at the beginning when it was still in fragments.

My mother died when I was a year old. My father, who was a rubber planter in Malaya, was taken prisoner of war by the Japanese. As a child I did not know either of them. I was sent home and brought up by an Aunt and Uncle in a small village on the west coast of Scotland where my Uncle was a Presbyterian minister. We lived in a large, bleak manse with three pianos, an organ, a bottled tarantula, porridge, twenty hens, and a black engine which made our own electricity. The house was very cold and icicles hung from the ceilings like crystal chandeliers. The gray black colors of the Manse seemed to symbolize my faith at that time.

My uncle's study was dark. Papers and sermons lay on the floor in disarray, and the desk was piled with rusty pennies, bottled scorpions, dried lizards, prune stones, and homemade treacle toffee that looked like black broken glass. Around the library shelves were obscure and unreadable books, flyblown and cobwebbed together. In one corner of the room was a church organ, ceiling-high, with huge gray pipes deep breathing like a giant. My uncle loved thick pimply porridge that he insisted on cooking himself on a primus stove, which sent volcanic flames three feet into the air. As for religion, I cannot remember much about the Gospels. I remember only the darkest bits of the Old Testament: the plague of locusts, the plague of darkness, and burning in the lowest Hell. "The sword without, the terror within shall destroy both the young man and the virgin, the suckling also with the man of gray hairs." "And Moses stretched his hand towards heaven, and there was thick darkness in all the land of Egypt, and for three days they saw not one another."

My uncle was a kindly man but often remote. Although optimistic by nature, he always responded in a voice of doom to the things I really wanted to know about and understand. He had won the Military Cross for bravery in the trenches during the First World War. He had read Divinity at St. Andrews University in Scotland and had been a scratch golf player, still driving golf balls from the vegetable garden high over the rookery into the graveyard beyond. My aunt seemed weighed down by circumstance, such as the war and rationing and too little help. She was always ill, overworked, tired, and anxious in a house that was too large and too inconvenient to manage. She was educated at Cambridge University but her face, once beautiful and alert, had become etched cruelly as bitterness and the cold set in. It was an unhappy and lonely childhood with little to lighten it except the beauty of the Scottish rivers and the larch forests.

As an exercise I have often tried to re-enter this period of my life with the knowledge that I have now and not with the limited vision of childhood. But this is like forcing a piece of the puzzle into the wrong place.

We were caught in a Scottish Presbyterian and rather stark culture, not completely fanatic but bound by many restrictions. Although the root of religion must have been planted in my subconscious, I rejected it because it emanated so little joy.

Every Sunday I sat in the front pew of church on a prickly horse hair cushion. I listened to my uncle's sermons all through childhood and never heard a word.

When I was nineteen, my father returned from being a prisoner of war in Malaya. We left for London, where I was to study music, and attempted to live together as two strangers.

I was confirmed in the Anglican Church, probably because most of my friends were now Anglican and as a revolt, perhaps, from my Scottish upbringing. I don't think there was a particularly "deep" reason. I may have expected some sort of guidance or awakening, but either I was closed intellectually or God chose not to reveal Himself until much later. My instruction remains a theological blank.

I married into the Establishment and lived, with all the predictable trappings of the upper classes, in my husband's sixteenth century Manor House in Wiltshire. God was now like a Patron's name on a letter heading. You knew He was important but nobody had introduced you. Religion (for us in the 1960s) was an accepted, rather formal obligation, something external, on a social, moral and national level. We sat up straight in a crested pew of our village church. The church was huge, like a cathedral. We sang hymns lustily and listened to the weekly sermon. Private prayer, when you lowered your head among the hymn books and usually made a hurried list of requests on a superficial level, was a self conscious moment before the service began. I don't think you were expected to pray deeply. People would have stared in astonishment. There was no mystery or stillness, the natural environment through which God could act. Inspiration depended on the eloquence of the sermon or the loudness of the hymn singing. Sometimes a seed was sown but it seldom germinated. "Entertainment" on a more radical level with acoustic guitars and hand-clapping had not yet entered into public worship. I seldom, if ever, found that feeling that we know in Orthodoxy of being in the undiluted awesome holiness of His presence.

Britain is filled with beautiful churches and cathedrals built and dedicated to God. But few people have the courage to talk about Him. Try talking about God at an English dinner party and watch the faces glaze in silent disbelief. Unless used in the context of satirical allusion it will be a social gaffe guaranteed to obliterate all credibility.

Perhaps we do not have enough symbolism for the seeds of living theology to be planted deep into our souls. Religion is established, yet our education accepts only what is visible. To believe in the invisible is almost impossible. We are too rational, too cynical, educated for legality, pragmatism, facts, and proof. Our thinking is closed and incompatible with the divine nature.

For some years I let such observations remain dormant as energies went into bringing up a family. But from 1960 onwards, when we experienced a series of unexpected tragedies, I began to see that my secular and superficial faith was totally inadequate.

At the end of this period, and because of the serious financial difficulties in keeping up a large house, the Manor had to be sold. It wasn't simply the sale of a family house. We had to see what seemed centuries of indestructible tradition topple and fall as easily as a dead tree.

We had always kept white fantail pigeons. They strutted about the immaculate lawns with their chests puffed up so high that they fell over backwards, breeding so continually that we could never count how many we had. Suddenly they stopped breeding and their numbers decreased rapidly. Whether the cause was rats, cats, or poison we never learned. Finally, one white pigeon walked across the lawn. Within a week it had flown away like the spirit leaving the material body which can no longer contain it.

The next day we left. After owning large estates in Wiltshire for many years, our family suffered a death of everything that was familiar, a waste land of insolvency where no birds sing.

The *nouveaux* poor are as bad as the *nouveaux* rich because they do not know how to handle their situation and the two states are in constant collision.

By the following Easter we had moved to a much smaller Jane Austen town house in a walled garden. There were ring doves in the apple trees, ivy on the walls, and bluebells in the grass. Informality replaced grandeur.

My elder daughter Sarah gave us a housewarming present of a lily in a pot. We put it on the kitchen table so that we could watch it. The growth was slow, then it shot straight up in the air like a lamp post and divided into two. We laughed because for so long there had been no movement and now it was incongruous, neither one thing nor the other, a little like us. But it seemed to have a significance and we watched its growth with all the love that was left in us.

One day my youngest daughter Charlotte, came rushing to my bedroom carrying a broken stem. She was in tears. "Mummy, the lily has broken and it's bleeding." As she held it, a thick red substance oozed from the stem on to the palms of her hands. It may have been the sap of the lily, but it was the color and texture of blood. The stem was veined in scarlet. I told her not to worry because there was still another stem, and it would now be stronger to bear the flowers.

A few days later the three of us came into the kitchen just as the evening sun shone gold on to the lily. Three flowers had opened quite suddenly and almost instantaneously and we watched in stunned silence at the extraordinary sight in front of us. The lily was in the shape of a cross, a white and golden cross of unbelievable and unearthly radiance.

In May 1979 my husband was appointed Lord in Waiting to Her Majesty the Queen and on the same day my father died. Flowers came to the door, "Congratulations on your wonderful news." "Deepest sympathy in your sorrow." We were pulled apart like elastic, celebrating and mourning simultaneously.

Perhaps it was the start of a more permanent separation. During the last few years we had reacted to loss with two completely different sets of emotions. Three years later, after twenty six years of marriage, our separation became final.

Like many others in the West, my concept of Christianity was simplistic and rudimentary. I had never found theological reasons for dealing with the darker periods of our lives. Religion in its established presentation had provided no living experience; in fact, it seemed irrelevant to our complicated situation. I knew nothing about the lives of the Saints other than brief geographical histories that never came to life. A vital ingredient was missing. With a desperate thirst for Light and for Learning I set off on an isolated and very personal journey.

I see it now rather like an airplane taking off and flying through the subliminal turbulence of low cloud. It is bumpy and sometimes dangerous, yet through the darkness you see glimpses of clear blue sky. At this level you can experience visions, but without instruction you do not know how to discern. The soul is vulnerable in its natural freedom and openness, and perhaps I strayed too far, but I had a naive, built in trust in the power of goodness. Learning lessons on the way, I was eventually led out of the mist and phenomena into the transparency of the sky above. But it took several years.

Without the scaffolding and equipment of society I was reacting strongly to the presence of living things. It started with a simple observation of nature where every leaf, every wild flower, and every bird was engraved with the impact of sudden beauty. For many years they had been a background to living; now they were like infinite riches. I would stare with wonder and awe at an ivy leaf, the pattern of scales on a rainbow trout, a fallen flower petal, a blackbird, a dragon fly....

It is difficult to describe a mystical experience. Words reduce it. One sees something "ordinary" and learns something extraordinary. It all happens very quickly. You can't grasp or hold on to it, for it is like liquid flowing. The soul's perception is quickened and Love is part of it. Peace, joy (and again the words are inadequate) infuse over one's whole being as though one has entered a transfigured, timeless, and primordial state, as in the First Garden, perhaps, before Man and God became separated.

The more straightforward approach to God through the stories of the Gospels had for some reason simply not ignited a response in me. That was to come later, but not until I had found the Orthodox way of presenting Christianity. It seemed I had to start right from the beginning, learning and absorbing by osmosis rather than from words. The Light was undefined, yet I feel, on looking back, that God led me, as I'm sure He does all of us, according to my own particular capacity.

From the beauty and wonder of Nature I began to learn about the abstract. I remember, for instance, observing the garden poppy. When it flowers it is scarlet and flamboyant. Then the crumpled petals wither and fall away. There is a certain ugliness in the first death. It looks like the end, yet a few days later everything has changed. In the place where the petals have been there is a star-shaped lid, perfect in its mathematical precision and timing, holding the seeds of a new beginning. From this I grasped that life "continually assumes new forms" far in advance of our human intellect.

On three occasions my younger daughter Charlotte had said that she would die young. There was nothing neurotic or dramatic about her remark. It was simply a statement. I remember illustrating it with the same sort of analogy as the poppy. I told her never to be frightened of death. To think of it as change. Like a caterpillar changing into a butterfly.

These fairly simple observations, and there were hundreds of them, gradually led to ideas that became more complicated. It was not simply a search for knowledge for the sake of knowledge but a longing to reach God. The only way that seemed open to me was to understand His creation.

The stem of a jasmine, for instance, is unremarkable in itself, like dull green wire, yet it contains such potential beauty, clusters of green leaves with white five petalled scented flowers that are sheer magic. I began to grasp the potential held in all of us. The past, the present, and the future were already implicit. This led me to seeing Time, not simply as finite, but in its full eternal dimension. I realized that the soul was not confined to Space and Time but could, on occasions, resonate, or "home in" on much wider levels than is normally grasped by the five senses. I was, I suppose, at a gnostic, heretical stage, learning from revelation. It seemed that parallels to the most profound human situations could be made clear as I contemplated on the purpose of the more obscure natural phenomena from a hot spring to a piranha fish. Having seen such wonder and order in nature, I began to sense the disorder in the way in which people, so closed in soul that they were totally blind to the wisdom of God's creation, shot off in the wrong directions and with distorted emphases.

The evil in the world worried me. It was like a virus, a bacteria, a negation of all Light.

I began to have huge cosmic dreams showing the whole gamut of man's evil in the extremes, from the bizarre "over the top" decadence and headline depravity to the other extreme, the narrowing down mentality that reduces, with human logic, to automatic, impersonal reaction. Both have the purpose of breaking down. In Nature this is clarified, for the parasitical process is in itself part of nature. An unexpected flash of insight seemed to expand this particular theme beyond mere Dualism.

One day I was making a lemon soufflé, whisking the eggs and hoping that nobody would telephone or interrupt my concentration. There was a bluebottle flying around the kitchen which irritated me; I thought briefly of its apparent uselessness and considered it a typical, if trivial, example of the manifestation of evil in nature. I opened the door hurriedly to let it out and wrote down the following words before I could forget them: *The force of evil is necessary to the world of matter because matter has to be broken down. When this is understood only that which is necessary is broken down. When it is not understood the balance is tipped and there is chaos. In the realm of true spirit there is no evil because there is no matter.*

I saw therefore, that evil (or the breaking down process that destroys by negation) actually had a purpose in the destructive and regenerative forces of nature. Evil was maladjusted and unbalanced when it broke away and became separate. Not only were the extremes of evil, as discussed earlier, implicated in this concept, but evil involved all the negative and destructive traits of Man from cynicism to anger to domination and to all kinds and degrees of cruelty and aggression.

Although this was an accelerated time of learning, it was happening in a state of almost perpetual heightened consciousness that grew from stillness and, at the same time, alertness. I did not judge my sources of knowledge, I simply trusted that by being open to God's guidance I would know the ultimate reason for what I had to learn. I realized that "enlightenment" seldom arrived without some sort of awareness or preparation. It had to be preceded by a certain openness; if I transgressed "dogma," it was not a permanent transgression. Soon I would realize, from learning about God through nature, that He was at the same time beyond nature.

I certainly had a feeling of being prepared for something, and with what Jung refers to as synchronicity, I began to meet remarkable people who seemed to come into my life at exactly the right moment, as though to lead me out of one stage of understanding and into the next.

My religion, if one could call it that, was emanatory inasmuch as there are some people in whose presence we feel happier and stronger physically, and others whose negative vibrations and influence can actually destroy us. I was beginning to understand the presence of Christ Who in touching someone, either physically or spiritually, was able to comfort and heal by emanation, transmitting His own spiritual wholeness and love into that person. Just as one felt evil by proximity, so one experienced feelings of Holiness.

A passage in *Le Milieu Divin* by Teilhard de Chardin describes perhaps what was happening at this stage of my journey:

> *"I attain God in those who I love to the same*
> *degree in which we, myself and they, become more*
> *and more spiritual. In the same way I grasp Him*
> *in the Beautiful and the Good in proportion as I*
> *pursue these further and further with progres-*
> *sively purified faculties."*

If my faith was being built up in an almost miraculous way, then it was about to be tested.

My youngest daughter Charlotte had pulled on to the hard shoulder of the M.4 Motorway when the car she was driving had overheated. She was with a girlfriend, tanned and happy from her first holiday in Spain, shiny plastic bags filled with shells and presents. She had just rung me to say she'd be back for lunch. She never made it. A truck ploughed into her from behind, tearing off the roof of the car like a sardine tin. It was instant oblivion, an unnatural and very contemporary death, grotesque in its violence.

We sat by her still body in the Intensive Care Unit of the Princess Margaret Hospital in Swindon. She was wired into technology, flawless in her beauty, in spite of the deadly head and chest wounds. The smell of petrol permeated the area around her bed. We held her hands, we prayed, we sent beams of love, and each member of the family lived through a lonely agony, made bearable because it was unbearable in its magnitude.

A week later she was buried in the graveyard beside the old Manor where we used to live. Steeple Ashton is a small village in Wiltshire. The church, like a cathedral, was packed with people. Two days later there was another funeral shown on television. As an actress, Charlotte had just been making a name for herself. In a series called "Tripods" she played the daughter of a Count and Countess who was sacrificed to the Tripods and, in a hauntingly beautiful death scene, was raised into the sky for a new life in the City of Gold. There were too many coincidences....

If someone dies who is young and good and vital and beautiful and if you love her, there is no way you can accept that death is the end or that her loss is something other than very sacred. I now felt that the gifts I had received must be purified and verified and tested to the limits. There was no space for ambiguity, for the seeds that Charlotte had sowed in her short life had to be honored if her death was to make any sense at all. Perhaps this was the conversion point to my understanding that there had to be one Holy God who was absolute, infinite, loving, and eternal. Suddenly the Resurrection of Jesus Christ became terribly important.

The analogy of the butterfly was soon to have unforeseen implications. Charlotte had never been to Greece, yet her paintings during the few months before her death had taken on a strangely mystical quality. They showed classical landscapes that were almost paradisical. It was as though she had already touched a Holy Place. We followed the drawings and arrived in the Greek island of Aegina. There were three of us, my elder daughter Sarah, and John Tavener the composer, a close friend of us both. John's mother had died at about the same time as Charlotte.

One day a butterfly lay dead at Sarah's feet. It was the largest butterfly we had ever seen and striped like a dress that Charlotte wore. Sarah lifted it up gently because it seemed to symbolize Charlotte's death. We left the dead butterfly at the Monastery dedicated to St. Nectarios. We prayed and cried and felt a peace that passed all understanding at the little white church . Later as we lay on the beach I said it was strange that a butterfly, like a soul, was attracted to beautiful things - jasmine, hibiscus, oleander. It would never come to a beach to land on seaweed. But an exact replica of the enormous butterfly we had left with St. Nectarios hovered on the seaweed in front of us. Then it just flew away over the sea.

Our visit to the tomb of St. Nectarios had a profound effect on me. I knelt beside the cold marble where jasmine, white roses and camellias lay in profusion, sweet smelling and familiar.... There was a feeling of weightlessness, of timelessness, and of infinite grace. We lit a candle in the small courtyard. I had never lit a candle for anyone before. Charlotte's was the first, leaving a flame in the bright sunlight. White walls, black dresses, scarlet geraniums -- the colors of death and perpetual life.

I am more cautious now with anything that can be termed a vision but in the early evening as I lay resting in the white cell of my room, with the bougainvillea trailing over the arched window, I shut my eyes. And then I saw face after face of extraordinary beauty and purity, one dissolving into the next. They were Apostolic, Saint-like, Christ-like faces....

At night, to the sound of cicadas, we would eat against the flat biblical backcloth of the sea. The sun, as it went down looked spherical instead of flat, as though another dimension was creeping into our lives. We could have been beside the Sea of Genneseret. The fishermen and the fishes were there, and the symbolic bread and wine, always shared.

People here talked about God without inhibition. Macarios the Great, Gregory Palamas, John Damascene, Symeon the New Theologian, Basil the Great had never come into our conversation before. Suddenly we felt we had been deprived of so much spiritual teaching. Why had so little of the richness of this early Christian knowledge permeated into the West? Where were the writings of the Holy Fathers and of the Saints? Was it surprising that our faith felt so incomplete and diluted? Here there was both simplicity and scholarship and an electrifying living faith where we heard strong men talk about Angels as easily as an Englishman talks about the weather.

John was already Orthodox but Sarah and I flew from Athens to Heathrow each clutching an icon of St. Nectarios of Aegina, a plastic bottle filled with holy oil, *The Orthodox Way* by Bishop Kallistos and a book on the Desert Fathers.

I was unable to forget the impact of Orthodoxy. It drew me like a magnet. After returning home I heard about a small English speaking Orthodox parish very near to where I lived. With excitement and optimism I was soon knocking at the door of a new religion. But if I thought it was the end of a journey I was mistaken. It was simply the beginning.

My first book was due to be published. I had signed the contract and the story described my frantic search for God. The title, *Let the Petals Fall*, symbolized Loss. I took it from an Indian saying of the daily shedding of petals from the beautiful frangipani tree. The ground on which they lie is known as sacred ground. I had always felt that Loss had to be transfigured. Abundance and its stripping away had followed me throughout life. I had to make sense of Loss or my whole life was meaningless. The book was a very personal journey to the point of Orthodoxy. I had strayed in every direction, spanning it seemed Time and Space in my search for Truth, but I had touched on things that were an anathema to the dogma of the Orthodox Church and the doors of the Community closed. I felt separated not from a system but from God Himself.

One dark and very stormy day I stood before Charlotte's grave. A judgment, as lightning, forked through the black sky and rain fell like swords into the humped earth. I felt an irrational maternal urgency to protect her from the storm around us and from the new and unexpected storm in my life. Everything must be transfigured, made holy again. But how? The Manor where we had once lived was darkened with tears of rain. The church beside me, like a cathedral, was beautiful and gaunt. I remembered the crowds that had packed into it for her funeral. "Jerusalem" sung by so many voices was as a prophecy. There was something sacred and holy and innocent and full of love. Now it was empty. No flowers and no people. God had been everywhere and now was nowhere.

A rainbow appeared in the black sky, linking Heaven to Earth. A tall tree came alive with starlings, shimmering with light and sound. I couldn't see the beauty of the rainbow. Nor did I know whether the tree of life so close to me was good or bad. The desolation was too severe to discern anything.

Psychologically there was a dangerous void as the wound of confession lay unstitched and open to disintegration. It was wild and sinister, darkness and light mixed together. A Requiem with the tall tree shrieking. I thought of something written by Maurice Pagnall on this feeling of separation: "He died facing the enemy where he did not even know the names of the flowers."

For the next year or so I was in another no-man's-land, in an exile with a loss of identity where I belonged to nothing. The irony was that Orthodoxy called more strongly than ever. I felt like Gogol, the Russian writer, who discovered Christ at the end of his life and tried to alter all the books he had ever written. Some say he went mad in the process.

Rational friends gave advice: "You were better without the Church! You don't need a Church! You've got the wrong Church! Enjoy life! Be funny again, you used to be funny. Jesus Christ is a man made myth. If you turn the other cheek nowadays you won't have any face left."

I sat with an icon of Christ in front of me day after day. But my prayers were incoherent and broken.

Sarah, John Tavener, and Frances Meigh, a Catholic hermit, hovered like Guardian Angels, understanding the intensity and eventually starting to move what seemed like an immovable situation.

I shall never forget Christmas 1986. I had flu and a high temperature and was listening to the midnight broadcast from the Russian Orthodox Cathedral in London where the Vigil starts in darkness as the Hours are read. There is an excitement, an awesome expectation, before the Royal Doors are flung open, and the darkness gives way to Light with the singing of the words from Isaiah "God is with us!"

Then I heard the words of Metropolitan Anthony of Sourozh. "The Church is vast," he said. "So vast that it holds both Heaven and Earth. So vast that people of all nations, of all cultures, of all languages are its home." He spoke of God's infinite love, for the gift of His Son, for the salvation of each of us singly and for the whole of the world. "We are born into Time in order to grow into Eternity .... Let us receive whole-heartedly, daringly, faithfully the message of the Gospels" - and so on, in the extraordinary way that Metropolitan Anthony speaks, when the love of God infuses into every syllable. That he is known by many as the "voice of Orthodoxy" in Britain is understandable. The Light simply shone into the darkness.

Immediately after the long Vigil Sarah rang from London. Metro-politan Anthony came into the body of the Cathedral to look for her and asked to see us both. We each saw him in London, and he became our Spiritual Father, taking over our instruction into the Orthodox Church.

Metropolitan Anthony had already read my unpublished, unedited manuscript. He knew it was far from Orthodox but he knew, too, that it followed the personal path I had walked along and to which I would not return. One day he asked me for a copy of the book. I was very nervous. Before giving it to him, I took a pen and started to score out several paragraphs, writing notes in the margin. "Father Anthony, don't read this bit." "Miss this out." "You won't like this part," etc. He took the pen from my hand.

"What are you doing?" he said, "I love ALL of my spiritual children, not just bits of them!"

The Spiritual Father relationship is an essential part of the Orthodox tradition. A *starets* is the Russian word for a wise man. Because of his asceticism, discipline, and constant prayer he is a man of inward peace in whom the grace of the Holy Spirit exists and acts. In a man so close to God, the words are moved by God and "the sheep follow him for they know his voice."

But it is not just through his words that the change takes place. More often it is through his silence, prayer, and presence. He does not compel, but kindles, leading one to spiritual maturity. Arrogance moves into humility, and the belief in God is like a sword plunged into a fire. The steel and the heat become inseparable. Just as through Christ's Divinity we can see God, so in men that are Holy we can see Christ.

A final piece of the broken jigsaw puzzle fell into place. There was to be a concert of John Tavener's music in an Anglican church in London. One composition was dedicated to Charlotte, and I wondered if I would feel nostalgic for what I was leaving behind. But arriving at this beautiful church was like walking into a Fair Ground. It was decorated as a Rain Forest, but the unfortunate symbolism of palm trees with plastic parrots, snakes blown up like colored balloons, and what seemed like voodoo masks around the walls clashed so completely with the sacredness and purity of John's music that I felt no moment of regret.

The next day at the cathedral in Ennismore Gardens the Feast of Pentecost was being celebrated. Ivy trailed discreetly from above the Royal Doors. The simplicity and the beauty and the timeless rhythm of Eternity joined Heaven to Earth. The candlelight and the calm presence of the icons introduced a reality and hierarchy of such Holiness that faces, however plain in the worldly sense, were transfigured in prayer.

Sarah and I were each given a flower from a parishioner. It was customary to bring flowers and we had none with us. Mine was a daisy, too soon after Charlotte's death, for daisies had been such an important part of her funeral. I looked at my wilting flower. It symbolized too much. My life, perhaps. How could God transfigure something so flawed and imperfect. I couldn't hold it and, rather than throw it away, I gave it to Sarah. Hers was less flawed. It hid the imperfection of the flower that I was holding.

We knelt down for the long prayers of Pentecost when the Holy Spirit is invoked and descends onto the people. Suddenly I was blinded by glass. In the glass was the reflection of a perfect daisy, each petal intact and shining with immaculate illumination.

Only at the end of the liturgy did I turn round. The huge window in the cathedral is in the shape of a daisy. The sunlight had shone through with geometric accuracy on to the reflection that had blinded me. I have tried to find and repeat the same set of circumstances on many occasions since, but it has never happened again. It never does. God had given me His answer that He can transfigure anything, however flawed.

We were taken into the Orthodox Church in 1986 by Metropolitan Anthony and Father John Lee. It was the most true, most moving, most privileged, and most important event in my life.

If I have any regrets it is that I discovered Orthodoxy so late. If I have any wish it is that the maturity, the dignity, the disciplines, and the integrity of this great Christian Tradition could bring sacredness back into the West.

The Mirage Becomes a Pool
by Father Daniel Matheson

Nothing speaks as clearly to me of the vast mystery and blessing of my becoming an Orthodox Christian as the vision of Isaiah when he contemplated the deliverance of the Children of Israel and wrote -- or sang-- "The mirage becomes a pool".[13] Orthodoxy was a "mirage" for me through many wistful years: it was always on my horizon; I was drawn by the magnet of the "beauty of holiness" that I perceived there; I studied its asceticism, and comforted myself through many difficult days by quietly praying, "Lord Jesus Christ, Son of God, have mercy on me, a sinner." And now, at last, it has become my "pool": I have knelt, put my face into its waters, and drunk deeply. I am refreshed and fulfilled.

I had never made a secret of my intense interest in Orthodoxy -- even to the extent of advising my immediate family: my wife, our daughter, and our sons, that, as my discomfort in the United Church of Canada[14] became more acute, it had become a possibility as I looked at "catholic" options. However, there must have been something "unthinkable" about the fact of conversion, because when eventually my wife and I were received into the Orthodox Church we were astonished at the distress our action caused.

Through God's grace my wife, Vera, who is very different from me, arrived at Orthodoxy about the same time as the doors began to open for me. I had hungered for Orthodoxy for years; Vera was convinced after one exposure to the divine liturgy! This was anything but typical of other familial reactions: our sons and daughter found our conversion difficult and embarrassing. Many of our less immediate relatives and our friends must have been deeply shocked, for their relationships with us became stiff, formal, and politely reserved -- as if we had done some unmention-

---

13   Isaiah 35:7 *(New English Bible)*

14   The United Church of Canada is a union of Presbyterians, Methodists, and Congregationalists. The original union was in 1925; other smaller denominations entered the union later. It is the largest Protestant church in Canada.

able thing that must be overlooked. Rightly or wrongly, people seem to have expectations of each other, and we had profoundly disappointed just about everyone we knew.

In the end, our daughter came through with the radical truth; she said, "The mistake was that you were ever anything else; you have always been Orthodox!"

✠ ✠ ✠ ✠ ✠ ✠

I was born into a Presbyterian family on Epiphany, 1916. The word "Epiphany" meant nothing at all in our home: my mother always referred to the day as "old Christmas." When I was exactly three months old I was baptized in St. Columba Presbyterian Church. I have no idea how my ancestors conceived of the patronage of St. Columba, but this reality may well have been my first influence toward Orthodoxy. "Who was St. Columba?" was one of my earliest questions, and I am quietly convinced that his prayers have helped to bring me home. In any event, the fact of St. Columba combined with the graves of my ancestors in the churchyard and their corresponding portraits in our home combined to give me a partial, but powerful, awareness of the Communion of Saints. They were always a part of me.

Because of these things I cannot recall a time when I was not aware of God: private prayer, family prayers, and public worship were always a part of my life. Our church had seen many of its sons enter the ministry, and I remember knowing when I was four years old that, more than anything else, I wanted to be a part of their company.

However, the work of the ministry seemed to be completely out of the question for me: I had a very serious speech problem and the thought of a stuttering minister was ludicrous. Instead I studied accounting, believing that it would enable me totally to avoid public speaking. I was, of course, bitterly frustrated as an accountant. One day another young accountant in the office put me forever into his debt: he said, "You know, you shouldn't be doing this at all; you should be a minister." "It's what I really want to do," I stammered, "but how can I do that with this voice?" Then he made a most important statement: "I shouldn't be surprised if your voice might not turn out to be one of your greatest assets." He gave me hope!

by Father Daniel Matheson

Speech therapy in Nova Scotia in 1934 was unheard of; so, immediately, I organized my own program of reading Milton and Shakespeare aloud and alone. I also began to answer the telephone at every opportunity -- for me, a very difficult thing to do.

Eventually I learned to manage my voice remarkably well and began the typical educational requirements for ordination in the United Church. This meant taking a degree in Arts with a heavy emphasis on Classical Greek and Philosophy, followed by three years of seminary with strongest emphasis being given to Systematic Theology, Homiletics, Old Testament, and New Testament. We studied Church History but it did not have a very high profile. Later on, after I had discovered my need, I did some post-graduate work on Patristics and Sacramental Theology.

In 1942 I was married and ordained. We were sent into the Canadian North where I served a mission in an area comprising a gold mining town and a scattered population of Crees, Objiways and Salteaux. Vera taught in the one room school that the mining town provided for the native children. There were no roads into this area: we had a choice of being flown in or taking the water route of rivers, lakes and long portages over corduroy[15] roads. For parts of the year, spring and fall, we were completely isolated due to the fact that the lakes and rivers were breaking up or freezing. We lived in a cabin that we used to describe as being "two rooms and a path!" The wilderness was beautiful, vast and so quiet that we could hear nothing but the sounds of the forest. These are not difficulties when one is young, newly married, and very much in love!

But nothing could save us from the culture shock. The mining town was rough, and the native settlement was more primitive than what we now identify as "Third World." There was almost no interest in the Church -- which, in a sense, did not exist: we had no buildings and only a minuscule corps of confirmed persons. I simply could not find any way to relate to the miners or the natives. We were the sixth couple the Church had sent in in ten years, and we, too, were plainly inadequate to the challenge. These were "war years," and I had asked for something really difficult: I got more than I bargained for!

The components of a "moment of truth" are often unpredictable and inexplicable, and I have never understood why the lonely death of one neglected native child should have shaken me so deeply: it happened in

---

15   A corduroy road is made by laying logs side by side across a muskeg (i.e. a kind of northern bog).

September and my profound discomfort began. It came to a head at Easter when I found I could not prepare an honest Easter sermon, and, deeply agitated, I confessed to my wife that the only part of the resurrection Gospel that had meaning for me was Mary Magdalene's lonely cry: "They have taken away my Lord, and I know not where they have laid Him."

It would be unfair to lay the blame for this loss of faith totally on the door-step of my liberal seminary: not everyone lost his faith there. The truth is that somehow I had jettisoned my rural simplistic faith for a collection of intellectual theories. I could have written an essay on what all the contemporary Protestant theologians believed, but I, myself, simply did not have a belief. I was hundreds of frozen miles from any kind of counseling or guidance. I was, however, greatly blessed by the support of my wife and a handful of persons who loved me and talked down my desperate attempts to quit. Instead, I began to pray. My constant prayer went something like this: "Father, I know I belong to You through my Baptism, but I am totally confused about Jesus: help me!" A year later we moved to another church in a pleasant little town on the bleak prairie on the border of Manitoba and North Dakota; not surprising, there were no answers there, either. I prayed that lonely prayer for four years.

Eventually, we moved back to my native Nova Scotia and my wife introduced me to an Anglican evangelist, Canon Quintin Warner; he was one half of a mission team that was in our town for two weeks. I don't remember much about the sermons or studies that the missioners gave, but the mystery was that, when I was with Canon Warner, I was powerfully convinced of the absolute reality of Christ Risen and Regnant! My joy knew no bounds; my wilderness wanderings were over; I had entered the promised land of faith. Like the Children of Israel I had to "take" my promised land in stages, but in a very real sense my ministry began at this point. Of course, new difficulties also began!

Preaching is enormously important in churches of the Reformed traditions, and that fact fitted well with the re-discovery of my faith. I became an ardent preacher: I thought of it as my most important work. I was determined that no person in my congregation would be disappointed in what I was doing with his time.

Church worship was rather difficult. Despite the history of our parent churches, the United Church had a strong prejudice against what it called "written prayers." This fact was incongruous because our official liturgy, *The Book of Common Order*, was actually a very good book and not well used at all. Technically, we were a free church, and able to choose to use any material available, but the faithful believed they detected insincerity if the minister used what they called "someone else's prayers." My congregations were never totally comfortable with my liturgical practice, and I experienced much stress where I should have received comfort and strength.

The Ecumenical Movement was just then gaining momentum in Canada and it exercised a profound influence on my life. The Anglican Church in Canada and The United Church of Canada began seriously to discuss union. In actual fact it became a thirty-year exercise in frustration for most of the clergy and members in those denominations, but not for me: I learned to love the Anglicans and the *Book of Common Prayer.* Believing, now, very sincerely in the value of the historical liturgical life of the Church, I began to study liturgy. Perhaps *The Shape of the Liturgy* by Dom Gregory Dix was the strongest single factor in my development. It was here that I first learned of the Divine Liturgy of St. John Chrysostom. It wasn't easy to locate a copy of that liturgy, complete with rubrics, but eventually I did. In fact, of course, I found some of the prayers I had been using, but I loved all of it, and wished with all my heart that I could use it for my celebrations. This, of course, was totally unthinkable! But I could, at least, do everything in my power to develop a strong, good liturgical life in my denomination. In fact, I was able to accomplish a surprising amount in this field: the United Church was busy revising its liturgy and I was part of the team that eventually produced the *Service Book* used in that church today. I find it strangely amusing now to attend a wedding or funeral in a United Church and hear "my" words coming at me in this context!

One of the strange quirks of my career in the United Church was that at the height of my involvement in the *Service Book* I was given an honorary Doctor of Divinity degree by the United Theological College of Montreal. I was delighted: "Here," I thought, "at last, the Church is recognizing the value of a strong liturgical life!" Consider my surprise when the citation turned out to be a tribute to my pastoral work! The actual benefit of this was in that it made me realize that the various events that I had so often seen as interruptions in my preaching and liturgical ministry were, in fact, valuable components, and for the remainder of my ministry I tried to keep these three realities in balance.

The Ecumenical Movement was very important in my life for quite a different reason: I came to know Christians of almost every variety from the Salvation Army through to Roman Catholics. How did I miss getting to know the Orthodox -- especially when I respected their liturgy so profoundly? The answer, of course, is that persistent problem: culture! We whose native tongue is English can be so stubborn about language! But God moves in mysterious ways: during these mid-years in my ministry five remarkable things happened.

First, a Jesuit friend in Toronto, knowing of my interest and involvement in the liturgical life of my church, invited me to attend a mass in his college. He explained that the mass would be in English instead of Latin, and that the liturgy would be the Divine Liturgy of St. John Chrysostom celebrated by a Melkite priest. It was to be an unforgettable memory! I grieved that I could not receive the gifts, but I can think of nothing more appropriate to say of this experience than to borrow some lines from Milton:

> *" ...in service high and anthems clear,*
> *as may, with sweetness in mine ear,*
> *dissolve me into ecstasies*
> *and bring all heaven before mine eyes!"*

The second event happened on one occasion when my wife and I were in New York. Some Russians we met in the Metropolitan Museum of Art invited us to attend vespers with them. I understood not a word, but the reverent beauty and prayerful deportment of the community awakened in me a sense of the holy that I had never experienced before. I remember the old men and women lighting candles, crossing themselves, and kissing the icons, and wishing I were a part of it. I had seen, at last, the face of the Christian East, and it was beautiful.

The third influence came when I was trying to improve my proficiency in the French language. I borrowed a book from a French-Canadian Roman Catholic nun: the book was *Le Pelerin Russe*. I was deeply moved as I traveled with "le pelerin" and contemplated his simple prayer, "Lord Jesus Christ, Son of God, have mercy on me, a sinner." It didn't take me long to find the English translation, *The Way of the Pilgrim*, but, most of all, the "Jesus Prayer" became my quiet inner prayer. Of course, this drove me into bookstores, and I began to find Orthodox books, especially those of the Metropolitan Anthony Bloom, and one vital book, The Monk of Mount Athos. These books became the nucleus of a collection of books on Orthodox prayer life that grew steadily from year to year.

The fourth influence came when I read in the Art section of our city paper, that a local artist, Michael O'Brien, a devout Roman Catholic, was showing his icons in the Ukrainian Orthodox Church Hall. As it happened, I practically ran to the exhibition on the last day with only about a half hour before closing. There weren't many persons there, and I had a very quiet, beautiful time wandering around contemplating the icons. As I was leaving I happened to notice an area I had missed, and as I turned I was confronted by an icon of the Theotokos. For the first time I realized the impact of her love, her obedience, and her beckoning hand drawing me to my Saviour. I burst into tears -- thankfully realizing that I was totally alone. I knew that I wanted to live with this icon for the rest of my life. Reverently, I lifted the icon from the wall and went looking for Michael! I knew what I was going to do with the icon: it was going to hang on the wall above my desk; I knew that in some remarkable way I had found a Mother in Heaven, but how in the world was I going to relate to her?

The fifth event took place quite unexpectedly one day in my study in the church. My door burst open without any knock or announcement of any kind. I was surprised, shocked, and alarmed when a man came in: he was drunk and dirty with blood on his hands and clothing. He was no stranger. Indeed, he was well known in the city and had a reputation for violence and grossly indecent behavior. He had quite a record and I certainly did not aspire to be part of his case history. In fact, he was looking for someone else. In this condition there was nothing I could do for him, and, eventually, I "talked" him out of the room and the church. How he had picked on that church, and how he had found his way to my study, will always be a mystery. What surprised me was that when he came through the door I found my right hand coming up to my forehead and realized that I was crossing myself. This was a totally new, totally unfamiliar action; of course, I didn't get the fingers right! When my surprise guest left, I found myself still wondering how such a thing could have happened to me of all people! I concluded that it was a gift from God -- one that I must keep and use for the rest of my life.

During all these experiences I was a hard-working minister with a large congregation and a larger than average staff. I was uncomfortable about some aspects of my church life, but I accepted that as inevitable: nothing in this world is perfect. I had no thought of leaving the United Church: it was my home - my family. I had been born into this tradition; my family and friends were all in this church; anything else was unthinkable. What did develop was that our congregational life became more "catholic." We had weekly celebrations of the Holy Communion and a greater use of the hymns and prayers of the ancient church -- East and West. My vestments became less "reformed," more "catholic." Icons, crosses, and candles found their way into the church; and not always through my initiative; I had good reason to believe that my leadership in this direction was having some effect. The United Church was already a church of mixed traditions, and it professed to believe in and to be working toward the union of all Christians. I believed that what I was doing was both natural and right -- if not always popular.

My "love affair" with Orthodoxy did not cease, but it was totally academic: I read Orthodox books and prayed some Orthodox prayers; I became a friend of the Lebanese grocer across the street; but, strangely enough, I had never met an Orthodox priest. I knew that I would like to have been born Orthodox, but becoming Orthodox was as unthinkable as changing my height or the color of my eyes.

During these years, however, and for other than congregational reasons, I was becoming very uncomfortable in my church. The religious struggles I had experienced in the first years of my ministry had made me a conservative in my theology, and the United Church was becoming more liberal and trendy every year. Belief in the Virgin Birth had become optional at best -- maybe quaint. I felt that the theology of the Incarnation was being attacked. A former moderator of our church wrote articles in one of our newspapers denying the Resurrection of Christ and the hope of everlasting life: I began to react in pulpit and press. Theologically, the real "crunch" came when our church courts side-stepped the affirmation of the Lord Jesus Christ as the King and Head of the Church. It is not surprising that the moral insights of the church also took a new turn. The United Church had been embarrassingly moralistic. When I was ordained it was a serious sin to drink a glass of beer; by the time I had been ordained thirty years the same church was supporting abortion on demand -- and much more! In all of this I was anything but inactive: I was part of every reform movement that I could find.

by Father Daniel Matheson

The inevitable happened. My discomfort in the United Church was probably less acute than their discomfort with me! I was constantly involved in some kind of defensive action. I, myself, was becoming an issue, and that was worse than unfortunate. I had been twenty years in my parish, and it made sense that I should move. My heavy secret, shared only with my wife, was that I knew we were not only leaving the parish, we were leaving the denomination. I had not the faintest idea where we would go or what we would do.

I am a rather emotional and traditional person and I was leaving hundreds of years of church and family history in Canada and Scotland. I used to joke about the fact that every time the church door opened someone from our family was either going in or coming out: now I was going out for the last time. I had no idea how Vera or our daughter or our sons would handle whatever it was that I would do -- and I didn't know myself what that would be.

And there was my parish! Twenty-one years of my ministry had gone into this congregation -- seven-hundred and fifty families -- and I knew everyone by their first names. I had baptized, confirmed, married, and buried hundreds of the members of these families; I had rejoiced with them and wept with them. Most poignantly, I had tried to lead them into a deeper life of sacramental worship and prayer, and I was trying to deal with the fact that they just weren't interested in my intentions. I can honestly say that I loved them all and most of them loved me, but being loved had never been my goal. Even to recollect the pain of this separation now after almost a decade is to experience again the bitterness of my grief.

I knew I wanted to be within the "catholic" tradition. My ecumenical experiences and the many acts of kindness that I was receiving from Christians of almost every persuasion had truly cleansed me of any prejudice I had ever had against other denominations. I was attracted to the "catholic" churches partly because I had become sensitive about the Apostolic nature of the Church, and I believed myself to be outside it. Equally important was the fact that I found the "catholic" type of church to be more loving than the "reformed," "evangelical" or "charismatic." It appeared that I didn't really fit very well in any category! Besides, I wasn't deaf and I could still read! The Anglicans and Romans were making statements that sounded suspiciously like the ones I had reacted against in the United Church. In the end I settled into an Anglican church while I waited for guidance. It was a very loving parish, and I shall always be grateful to them for the healing warmth we found there. But it wasn't easy: It is painful to have to stand and repeat, "...I believe in the Holy Catholic Church ..." and to realize that one is outside it.

About this time I met one of the (then)[16] bishops of the Evangelical Orthodox Church. My first reaction was, "Well, there's a contradiction of terms if ever there was one!" But I was intrigued. "Are you canonical?" was my first question. His answer was candid, honest, and intriguing: "No, we aren't, but we are trying to become canonical." I borrowed his service book and it was "orthodox" enough to awake my interest. There was apparently no end to my questions. The nearest parish in Canada was two thousand miles away in Saskatoon; the nearest in the United States was about one thousand miles away in Gary, Indiana: this didn't sound like a very good option! My wife and I decided to visit the Saskatoon parish. The experience convinced us of one thing, that if we lived in that city we would want to be a part of that church. But one parish might not be a good indication of a denomination -- however small the denomination was. I was given permission to attend a synod meeting in the Chicago area where I met other clergy and some of the (then) bishops. I knew that I had found the most like-minded clergy that I had ever experienced.

But when I returned home it all seemed to be far away and not relevant to our situation: a thousand miles is a considerable distance. No one wants to be that lonely in his church life!

I was reasonably happy in my unofficial Anglican connection. Some of my friends talked to me about becoming an Anglican. They knew of my interest in Orthodoxy and assured me that I could be as "orthodox" as I liked within the Anglican communion, but I suspected that one could be almost anything else, too! Besides, the prayer book, beautiful as it was, was not the divine liturgy. I thought about the Evangelical Orthodox Church and their longing to be received into canonical Orthodoxy: they were all really in just about the same situation as I was. They had been together about ten years, but it had taken the Church in Uganda about fifty years to find their way into Orthodoxy. I certainly didn't have that many years!

---

16 In 1986, when *Journeys to Orthodoxy* was being edited, the fate of the Evangelical Orthodox Church had yet to be decided. The interested reader must wait for a history of this fascinating event to be written. Suffice it to say that the Evangelical Orthodox Church, flourishing and mighty in missionary zeal, is now affiliated with the Antiochian Archdiocese.

Then one day I was sitting in my study reading the Church Fathers, I think it was St. Gregory of Sinai, and I was caught by one sentence: "Become what you are!" I knew that was exactly what I had to do. I had left the United Church because, to borrow a metaphor from Bonhoeffer, "it was like being on a train heading for the edge of a cliff and trying to save oneself by running down the aisle toward the back of the car." I saw the opposite in the Evangelical Orthodox Church: here was a train heading East to places like Antioch and Constantinople, and more importantly, toward Pentecost! Not likely it would be a fast train, and most probably I would die en route, but I would, at least, be headed in the right direction!

I was received by the Evangelical Orthodox Church in November, 1985. I had accidentally found myself leading a Bible-study group of a few persons who were, like myself, unhappy and frightened with the direction of the so-called mainline churches. They had already been asking me for more than Bible study; and they wanted a sacramental ministry. They became my tiny parish. I wanted to give my parish everything I had, so I started by giving them my birthday: we became Holy Epiphany Evangelical Orthodox Mission. I took an old linen table-cloth that had been a part of my great-grandmother's trousseau and converted it into an altar-cloth, and in the "icon corner" of our living room we began to realize the beauty of the fact that "we had seen the true light, we had received the Heavenly Spirit; we had found the true faith, worshipping the undivided Trinity; for He had saved us."

Actually my journey to Orthodoxy turns out to be rather different from the other persons who came in through the Evangelical Orthodox Church. Mine had been largely a private search; in fact, less a search than a revelation. How richly God has blessed us! It was part of God's gracious leading that had brought me into contact with these other priests practically on the eve of their and my entrance into the Holy Orthodox Church. They had labored, and I had "entered into their labors." I am profoundly indebted to them.

I was most fortunate in that I was one of the priests sent to the Antiochian Orthodox Archdiocesan Center when we accepted the Metropolitan Philip's invitation to come to him and make ourselves known. The results of that encounter are history. He could hardly have known how intense was our longing to be within the Orthodox fold. Personally speaking, he could hardly have laid down conditions that I would not try to fulfill. We wondered what he would demand of us. In fact, it became rather the reverse: it was what he offered us that moved us profoundly. We were hardly prepared for the awareness that our journey to Orthodoxy was almost over. None of us will ever forget the joy and relief we experienced when we heard His Eminence say, "Welcome Home!"

On the 21st of March, 1987 my wife and I were chrismated in Holy Resurrection Orthodox Church, Gary, Indiana, and I was ordained sub-deacon and deacon. The following day, in St. John Chrysostom Orthodox Church in Fort Wayne, His Grace Bishop Antoun ordained me to the priesthood. I was home at last! I was seventy-one; but it was the first day of spring!

How graciously God has illumined our way with beauty! After we returned home to Ottawa, the same Sister who years before had given me *Le Pelerin Russe* heard that I had become an Orthodox priest and that I was serving the liturgy in our apartment. She invited us to use the chapel in their convent, Maison Jeanne d'Arc. This became our "church home." Here, with my little band of converts, we explored and discovered the beauty of living and worshipping in the Orthodox way.

In January of 1991 I retired from full-time work and was appointed to serve as assistant priest in St. Elijah Orthodox Church in Ottawa. Here, at last, the curtain of culture has been penetrated: what a thin curtain it is! Orthodoxy is Orthodoxy whatever the language of the liturgy; there is, after all, "one Lord, one Faith, one Baptism."

People never ask me questions about what we have done; but there are a couple of questions I would like to be asked.

First: How do I feel now? Actually, I only have one negative experience: I am continually distressed and embarrassed by the jurisdictional separation. I was deeply into Orthodoxy before I realized that such a thing existed, and I find that non-Orthodox persons perceive it to be denominationalism. It is difficult to witness to the unity of Orthodoxy. I feel like a brother to all Orthodox, and I would like to experience this reciprocated. Despite this, I am totally fulfilled and happy. I am privileged to stand at Christ's altar and to be His priest, I am privileged to hear the confessions of my brothers and sisters and to declare God's loving forgiveness. I am privileged to be enabled to give Christ's Body and Blood to men, women, and children who hunger and thirst after right-eousness, and if they aren't hungering and thirsting, I have the joy of encouraging that hunger.

by Father Daniel Matheson

I have the privilege of enabling Christ's people to realize their salvation through the manifold mysteries of His Church.

Second, would I do it again? It is difficult to answer this with any kind of assurance. The truth is that if we could have foreseen the distress that our conversion caused in our relatives, and the loss of our friends, we just might not have had the courage to go through with it. We are not young, and probably this is more acute for us than it would be for younger persons. On this side of the move, however, it was abundantly worth while. God is good: He provides the grace we need in the difficult passages of life. His fullness overflows to fulfill our emptiness.

Since we left the United Church that body has been facing even more painful challenges to its faith and values. The exodus of ministers and members has accelerated -- and will almost certainly continue to do so. We were fortunate to have made our exit alone. I am sure it was easier to find God's direction that way.

After all, Christians should not complain about alienation: for us, it is "the name of the game." Did not the Holy Family have to flee into Egypt? Did not Christ have to flee from Nazareth? Did He not weep over Jerusalem? Was He not crucified outside the walls? Does not the New Testament describe our role in terms of "strangers," "aliens," and "pilgrims?" "Here we have no continuing city," but when I enter His Temple and exalt the Holy Gospel which is the Icon of Christ and proclaim the blessedness of the Kingdom of the Holy Trinity, I experience the majesty, light, and love of my eternal home.

Strange Yet Familiar
by Bishop Kallistos of Diokleia

> Heaven and earth are united today.
> *Hymn from the Vigil on Christmas Eve*

> O strange Orthodox Church!
> *Father Lev Gillet*

An absence and a presence

I can remember exactly when my personal journey to Orthodoxy began. It happened quite unexpectedly one Saturday afternoon in the summer of 1952, when I was seventeen. I was walking along Buckingham Palace Road, close to Victoria Station, when I passed a nineteenth-century Gothic church, large and somewhat dilapidated, that I had never noticed before. There was no proper notice-board outside it – public relations have never been the strong point of Orthodoxy in the Western world! – but I recall that there was a brass plate which simply said "Russian Church."

As I entered St. Philip's – for that was the name of the church   at first I thought that it was entirely empty. Outside in the street there had been brilliant sunshine, but inside it was cool, cavernous and dark. As my eyes grew accustomed to the gloom, the first thing that caught my attention was an absence. There were no pews, no chairs in neat rows; in front of me stretched a wide and vacant expanse of polished floor.

Then I realized that the church was not altogether empty. Scattered in the nave and aisles there were a few worshippers, most of them elderly. Along the walls there were icons, with flickering lamps in front of them, and at the east end there were burning candles in front of the icon screen. Somewhere out of sight a choir was singing. After a while a deacon came out from the sanctuary and went round the church censing the icons and the people, and I noticed that his brocade vestment was old and slightly torn.

My initial impression of an absence was now replaced, with a sudden rush, by an overwhelming sense of presence. I felt that the Church, so far from being empty, was full – full of countless unseen worshippers, surrounding me on every side. Intuitively I realized that we, the visible congregation, were part of a much larger whole, and that as we prayed we were being taken up into an action far greater than ourselves, into an undivided, all-embracing celebration that united time and eternity, things below with things above.

Years later, with a strange shock of recognition, I came across the story of St. Vladimir's conversion, recorded in the *Russian Primary Chronicle*. Returning to Kiev, the Russian envoys told the Prince about the Divine Liturgy which they had attended in Constantinople. "We did not know whether we were in heaven or on earth," they said. "We cannot describe it to you: of this alone we are sure, that God dwells there among humankind. For we cannot forget that beauty." I started with amazement as I read those words, for such exactly had been my own experience at the Russian Vigil Service in St. Philip's, Buckingham Palace Road.[17] The outward setting lacked the splendour of the tenth-century Byzantium, but like St. Vladimir's emissaries I too had encountered "heaven on earth." I too had felt the immediacy of the celestial Liturgy, the closeness of the angels and the saints, the uncreated beauty of God's Kingdom. "Now the powers of heaven worship with us invisibly" (The Liturgy of the Presanctified Gifts).

I left the church before the service had ended, and as I emerged I was struck by two things. First, I found that I had no idea how long I had been inside. It might have been only twenty minutes, it might have been two hours; I could not say. I had been existing on a level at which clock-time was unimportant. Secondly, as I stepped out on the pavement the roar of the London traffic engulfed me all at once like a huge wave. The sound must have been audible within the church, but I had not noticed it. I had been in another world where time and traffic had no meaning; a world that was more real – I would almost say more *solid* – than that of twentieth-century London to which I now abruptly returned.

---

17   It has long since been pulled down.

Everything at the Vigil Service was in Slavonic, and so with my conscious brain I could understand not a single word. Yet, as I left the church, I said to myself with a clear sense of conviction: *This is where I belong; I have come home.* Sometimes it happens – is it not curious? – that, before we have learnt anything in detail about a person, place or subject, we know with certainty: *This* is the person that I shall love, *this* is the place where I need to go, *this* is the subject that, above all others, I must spend my live exploring. From the moment of attending that service at St. Philip's, Buckingham Palace Road, I felt deep in my heart that I was marked out for the Orthodox Church.

I am grateful that my initial contact with Orthodoxy was not through reading books, nor yet through meeting members of the Orthodox Church in a social context, but through attending an act of worship. The Church, according to the Orthodox understanding, is primarily a liturgical community, which expresses its true self through invocation and doxology. Worship comes first, doctrine and discipline second. I was fortunate, then, to discover Orthodoxy first of all by participating in an act of corporate prayer. I encountered the Orthodox Church not as a theory or an ideology, but as a concrete and specific fact, as a worshipping presence.

"This is what I have always believed..."

In retrospect it is clear to me that my mind was already made up on that summer afternoon in 1952. Before being actually received, however, I waited for nearly six years. In Britain in the 1950s it was a highly unusual step for a Western person to seek entry into the Orthodox Church, and most of my English friends did their best to dissuade me. "You will be a lifelong eccentric," they objected. "God has set you culturally in the West; do not run away from the quandaries and the challenge of your historical inheritance." However beautiful Orthodox worship might be, was there not (they asked) a tragic gap between Orthodox principles and Orthodox practice? Was not my approach to Orthodoxy too idealized, too sentimental? Was I perhaps looking for a security and protection that we can never enjoy here on earth, and should not seek?

Less predictably, most of the Orthodox whose counsel I sought likewise offered me little encouragement. They were honest and realistic – and for this I remain grateful – in directing my attention to the historical shortcomings of the Orthodox Church, as well as to the particular difficulties it confronts in the Western world. There was much in Orthodoxy, so they warned me, that was very far from "heaven on earth"! When I approached the assistant bishop at the Greek Cathedral in London, Bishop James (Virvos) of Apamaea, he spoke to me kindly and at length, but urged me to remain a member of the Anglican Church in which I had been brought up. A Russian priest to whom I spoke in Paris gave me exactly the same advice.

At the time this puzzled me. In my reading about Orthodoxy I had quickly discovered that it claims to be, not just one among many alternative "denominations," but the true Church of Christ on earth. Yet it seemed as if the Orthodox themselves were telling me, "Yes, Orthodoxy is indeed the one true Church, but you should on no account join it. It is only for us Easterners, Greeks, Russians and the rest." Adherence to the saving truth appeared to depend on the accidents of birth and geography.

With hindsight I can appreciate better why Bishop James spoke as he did. Forty years ago there were many Orthodox, and also many Anglicans, who sincerely hoped that the Anglican communion would be reconciled to Orthodoxy in a corporate way. Individual conversions from Anglicanism to the Orthodox Church were therefore discouraged; Anglicans, it was felt, would do better to remain where they were, and to work for unity from within their present Church, acting as an "Anglo-Orthodox" leaven.

I fear that these hopes for corporate reunion were always unrealistic. But it has to be remembered that, during the first half of this century, the moderate "High Church" party within Anglicanism – which appeals to the Ecumenical Councils and the Fathers – was far stronger than it is today, whereas the extreme "liberal" tendency, with its doctrinal and moral relativism, was much less pronounced, although already plainly in evidence. At any rate Bishop James was by no means alone in his dream that High Anglicanism might eventually develop into the nucleus of a native-grown Western Orthodoxy.

Bishop James also had pastoral reasons. None of his parishes at that time used any English in their Sunday worship, and only a few of his clergy spoke anything but Greek. He was unwilling to accept British people into his care, lacking as he did the resources to look after them. In this he was surely in large measure justified; it is grossly irresponsible for Orthodox clergy to receive converts, and after that to do nothing further about them. (I can think of many cases where this has in fact happened....) Converts need to be integrated into a living community;

they should not just be thrown in at the deep end of the Orthodox swimming-pool, and then left to their own devices to sink or swim.

Besides this, as I now realize, Bishop James wished to test me. Seeing my eagerness to become Orthodox, he wanted me to look carefully at the arguments on the other side. He knew that, if I was serious, I would come back to him again. And so indeed it turned out.

Meanwhile, some time before I had gone to see Bishop James, I began to develop a variety of Orthodox contacts. Shortly after my first experience of Orthodox worship at the Russian church in London, I started my university course at Oxford. For four years I studied Classics – ancient Greek and Latin, with some modern philosophy – and then I stayed on at the university for two further years of theology. (Incidentally, I never went to Anglican theological college, nor was I ordained in the Church of England.) At Oxford I had the chance to meet Orthodox Christians at first hand. In particular I came to know Nicolas Zernov, the University Lecturer in Eastern Orthodox Culture, and I still recall with pleasure the generous hospitality dispensed by him and his wife Militza, and the exhilarating and unpredictable conversations that they used to initiate with their many guests. I also met Father (later Archbishop) Basil Krivocheine, who officiated at the small Russian chapel in Oxford, and who was preparing his classic edition of the *Catecheses* of St. Symeon the New Theologian. A new world opened up before me as I heard him read St. Symeon's description of his visions of the divine and uncreated Light, and I began to appreciate the central place assigned in Orthodoxy to the mystery of Christ's Transfiguration.

While at Oxford, under the influence of my close friend from school days, Donald (A.M.) Allchin, I became an active member of the Fellowship of St. Alban and St. Sergius, whose aim is to promote *rapprochement* between Orthodoxy and Anglicanism. The summer conferences of the Fellowship had a decisive effect on me. Here I listened to such Anglicans as Archbishop Michael Ramsey, Father Derwas Chitty, and Professor H.A. Hodges, all of whom regarded Orthodoxy as the integral fullness of the Christian tradition, to which Anglicanism needed to return. As they saw it, Anglicans could hold the full Orthodox faith while still remaining in the Church of England, and in this manner we could help to bring our fellow-Anglicans nearer to Orthodoxy.

Their enthusiasm fired my imagination, but a part of me remained unsatisfied. I longed to be Orthodox in a total and visible way. The more

I learnt about Orthodoxy, the more I realized: this is what I have always believed in my inmost self, but never before did I hear it so well expressed. I did not find Orthodoxy archaic, foreign or exotic. To me it was simple Christianity.

The Church is One

My early contacts with the Orthodox world were for the most part Russian. I devoured such books as *A Treasury of Russian Spirituality* by G.P. Feodotov, and *With the Russian Pilgrims to Jerusalem* by Stephen Graham. I was immediately attracted to St. Seraphim of Sarov, about whom I learned from Iulia de Beausobre's slightly fictionalized but deeply moving account *Flame in the Snow*. On the more theological level a crucial landmark in my journey was Alexis Khomiakov's short essay "The Church is One." Here I found, verbally expressed, that vision of the communion of saints which I had first experienced as a living reality at the Russian church in London:

> *The Church is one, notwithstanding her division, as it appears to a man who is still alive on earth.... Those who are alive on earth, those who have finished their earthly course, those who, like the angels, were not created for a life on earth, those in future generations who have not yet begun their earthly course, are all united together in one Church, in one and the same grace of God.... The Church visible, or upon earth, lives in complete communion and unity with the whole body of the Church, of which Christ is the head.... The Church, even upon earth, lives not an earthly life, but a life which is divine, and of grace.... There is one God, and one Church.*[18]

In later years, as I read more widely in Orthodox theology, I came to recognize the limitations of Khomiakov's Slavophil ecclesiology, but at the time he provided me with exactly what I needed. I was also greatly helped by Father Georges Florovsky's article, "*Sobornost:* the Catholic-

---

18   Alexis Khomiakov, "The Church is One," in W.J. Birkbeck (ed.), *Russia and the English Church during the Last Fifty Years* (London 1895), pp. 193-4, 211, 222.

ity of the Church," in which he emphasizes the essential nature of the Church as a unity-in-diversity after the image and likeness of God the Holy Trinity:

> *The realm of the Church is unity. And of course this unity is no outward one, but is inner, intimate, organic. It is the unity of the living body, the unity of the organism. The Church is a unity not only in the sense that it is one and unique; it is a unity, first of all, because its very being consists in reuniting separated and divided mankind. "It is this unity which is the 'sobornost' or catholicity of the Church." In the Church humanity passes over into another plane, begins a new manner of existence. A new life becomes possible, a true, whole and complete life, a catholic life, "in the unity of the Spirit, in the bond of peace" (Eph. 4:3). A new existence begins, a new principle of life, "even as Thou, Father, art in Me, and I in Thee, that they also may be in Us... that they may be one even as We are one" (John 17:21-23). This is the mystery of the final reunion in the image of the Unity of the Holy Trinity.*[19]

Catholicity, Father Georges adds, "means seeing our own self in another, in the beloved one";[20] and it is in the catholicity of the Church, and there alone, that "the painful duality and tension between freedom and authority is solved."[21] Throughout my later life I have constantly returned to this article, which says far more in twenty-one pages than most authors manage to say in whole volumes.

While it was chiefly from the Russians that I received my initial insight into Orthodoxy, during my first visit to Greece in 1954 the spiritual world of Byzantium also won my allegiance. As a Classicist my main purpose had been to look at the Acropolis, Olympia, Delphi and

---

19 Georges Florovsky, *"Sobornost:* the Catholicity of the Church," in E.L. Mascall (ed.), *The Church of God. An Anglo-Russian Symposium by Members of the Fellowship of St. Alban and St. Sergius* (London 1934), p. 55 (quotes in the original). This article is reprinted in Vol. 1 of Florovsky's *Collected Works* (Nordland, Belmont 1972).

20 *"Sobornost,"* p. 59.

21 *"Sobornost,"* p. 73.

Knossos. So, when my traveling companions included Sparta in our itinerary, I protested. Were not the Spartans mere gymnasts and militarists, who had left behind them no monument worthy of a detour? In fact what my friends were taking me to visit was not Sparta itself but the Byzantine town of Mistra three miles beyond. Here I was delighted to see before me not just a few scattered ruins but an entire city rising up the hillside – streets, palaces, monasteries, many-domed churches – all set against the spectacular back-drop of the snow-covered Taygetus range. Looking at the frescoed saints alive on the church walls, like W.B. Yeats I found in them "the singing-masters of my soul."

Tradition, Martyrdom, Stillness

As I deepened my knowledge of Orthodoxy, three things in particular attracted me and held me fast. First, I perceived in the contemporary Orthodox Church – despite its internal tensions and its human failings – a living and unbroken continuity with the Church of the Apostles and Martyrs, of the Fathers and the Ecumenical Councils. This living continuity was summed up for me in the words *fullness* and *wholeness*, but most of all it was expressed by the term *Tradition*. Orthodoxy possesses, not through human merit but by God's grace, a fullness of faith and spiritual life not to be found in any Western confession, a fullness within which the elements of dogma and prayer, of theology and spirituality, constitute an integral and organic whole. It is in this sense the Church of Holy Tradition.

In this context I would like to put especial emphasis on the word "fullness." Orthodoxy has the plenitude of life in Christ, but it does not have an exclusive monopoly of the truth. I did not believe then, nor do I believe now, that there is a stark and unmitigated contrast between Orthodox "light" and non-Orthodox "darkness." We are not to imagine that, because Orthodoxy possesses the fullness of Holy Tradition, the other Christian bodies possess nothing at all. Far from it; I have never been convinced by the rigorist claim that sacramental life and the grace of the Holy Spirit can exist only within the visible limits of the Orthodox Church. Vladimir Lossky is surely right to maintain that, despite an outward separation, non-Orthodox communities still retain invisible links with the Orthodox Church.

> *Faithful to its vocation to assist the salvation of all, the Church of Christ values every "spark of life," however small, in the dissident communities. In this way it bears witness to the fact that, despite the separation, they still retain a certain link with the unique and life-giving centre, a link that is – so far as we are concerned – "invisible and beyond our understanding." There is only one true Church, the sole bestower of sacramental grace; but there are several ways of being separated from that one true Church, and varying degrees of diminishing ecclesial reality outside its visible limits.*[22]

Thus on Lossky's view, which I willingly made my own, non-Orthodox communities continue in varying degrees to participate in the Church's life of grace. Yet it still remains true that, while these non-Orthodox communities possess *part* of the saving and life-giving truth, in Orthodoxy alone is the *fullness* of that truth to be found.

I was particularly impressed by the manner in which Orthodox thinkers, when speaking of their Church as the Church of Holy Tradition, insist at the same time that Tradition is not static but dynamic, not defensive but exploratory, not closed and backward-facing but open to the future. Tradition, I learnt from the authors whom I studied, is not merely a formal repetition of what was stated in the past, but it is an active re-experiencing of the Christian message in the present. The only true Tradition is living and creative, formed from the union of human freedom with the grace of the Spirit. This vital dynamism was summed up for me in Vladimir Lossky's lapidary phrase: "Tradition... is the *life* of the Holy Spirit in the Church."[23] Emphasizing the point, he adds: "One can say that 'Tradition' represents the critical spirit of the Church."[24] We do not simply remain within the Tradition by inertia.

---

22   Vladimir Lossky, introductory note to the article of Patriarch Sergius of Moscow, "L'Eglise du Christ et les communautés dissidentes," *Messager de l'Exarchat du Patriarche Russe en Europe Occidentale* 21 (Paris 1955), pp. 9-10.

23   My italics. See "Tradition and traditions," in Leonid Ouspensky and Vladimir Lossky, *The Meaning of Icons* (Olten 1952), p. 17; in the revised edition (St. Vladimir's Seminary Press, Crestwood 1982), p. 15. This essay is reprinted in Vladimir Lossky, *In the Image and Likeness of God* (St. Vladimir's Seminary Press, Crestwood 1974), pp. 141-68; see p. 152. Of course Lossky does not exclude the Christological dimension of Tradition, as is clear from the context in which this phrase occurs.

In the eyes of many non-Orthodox observers in the West, Orthodoxy appears as a Church of rigid immobility, oriented always towards the past. That, however, was not my personal impression when first I came to know the Orthodox Church in the early 1950s, and it is certainly not my impression today after being Orthodox for nearly forty years. Although many aspects of Orthodox life are indeed characterized by a certain archaism, that is very far from being the whole story. On the contrary, what Sir Ernest Barker says of the twelve centuries of Byzantine history can be applied equally to the nineteen centuries of Orthodox history: "Conservatism is always mixed with change, and change is always impinging on conservatism, during the twelve hundred years of Byzantine history; and that is the essence and fascination of those years.[25]

As the life of the Holy Spirit within the Church, so I discovered, Tradition is all embracing. In particular it includes the written word of the Bible, for there is no dichotomy between Scripture and Tradition. Scripture exists *within* Tradition, and by the same token Tradition is nothing else than the way in which Scripture has been understood and lived by the Church in every generation. Thus I came to see the Orthodox Church not only as "traditional," but also as Scriptural. It is not for nothing that the Book of the Gospels rests on the centre of the Holy Table in every Orthodox place of worship. It is the Orthodox rather than the Protestants who are the true Evangelicals. (If only we Orthodox in practice studied the Bible as the Protestants do!)

As the life of the Spirit, so Lossky and Florovsky assured me in their writings,[26] Tradition is not only all-embracing but inexhaustible. In the words of Father Georges Florovsky:

> *Tradition is the constant abiding of the Spirit and not only the memory of words. Tradition is a "charismatic," not a historical principle.... The grace-giving experience of the Church... in its catholic fullness... has not been exhausted either in Scripture, or in oral tradition, or in definitions. "It cannot, it must not, be exhausted."*[27]

---

24   "Tradition and Traditions," p. 19 (revised edition, p. 17).

25   Ernest Barker, *Social and Political Thought in Byzantium* (Oxford 1957), p. 28.

26   I had the happiness of knowing both of them not just through their writings, but personally: Vladimir Lossky before, and Father Georges after, my reception into the Orthodox Church.

27   "*Sobornost,*" pp. 65, 67 (quotes in original).

While the period of the seven Ecumenical Councils possesses a pre-eminent importance for Orthodoxy, we are not for one moment to imagine that the "age of the Fathers" came to a close in the eighth century. On the contrary, the Patristic era is open-ended. There is no reason – apart from human sin – why there should not be in the third millennium further Ecumenical Councils and new Fathers of the church, equal in authority to those in the early Christian centuries; for the Holy Spirit continues present and active in the Church as much today as ever He was in the past.

This vibrant and vivifying conception of Tradition that I discovered in Orthodoxy made increasing sense to me. More and more I found that the living continuity to which the Orthodox Church bore witness was lacking in the Anglicanism within which I had been brought up from early childhood. The continuity had been impaired, if not broken, by the deviations of the Latin West during the Middle Ages. Even if, for many Anglicans from the sixteenth century onwards, the English Reformation represented an attempt to return to the Church of the Ecumenical Councils and the early Fathers, how far in actual fact could this attempt be reckoned a success? The "Orthodoxy" of the Church of England seemed at best implicit – an aspiration and a distant hope rather than an immediate and practical reality.

I shall never cease to be sincerely grateful for my Anglican upbringing. Never would I wish to engage in negative polemic against the communion where I first came to know Christ as my Saviour. I remember with lasting happiness the beauty of the choral services in Westminster Abbey which I attended while a boy at Westminster School, and in particular I recall the great procession with cross, candles and banners at the Sung Eucharist on the feast of St. Edward the Confessor. I am grateful also for the links which I formed, while at school and university, with members of the Society of St. Francis such as Father Algy Robinson, the Father Guardian, and his young disciple Brother Peter. It was the Anglican Franciscans who taught me the place of mission within the Christian life and the value of sacramental confession.

I shall always regard my decision to embrace Orthodoxy as the crowning fulfillment of all that was best in my Anglican experience; as an affirmation, not a repudiation. Yet, for all my love and gratitude, I cannot in honesty remain silent about what troubled me in the 1950s, and today troubles me far more; and that is the extreme diversity of the conflicting beliefs and practices that coexist within the bounds of the Anglican communion. I was (and am) disturbed first of all by the contrasting views of Anglo-Catholics and Evangelicals concerning central articles of faith such as the real presence of Christ in the Eucharist and the Communion of Saints. Are the consecrated elements to be worshipped as the true Body and Blood of the Saviour? May we intercede for the departed, and ask the Saints and the Mother of God to pray for us? These are not just marginal issues, over which Christians may legitimately agree to differ. They are fundamental to our life in Christ. How then could I continue in a Christian body which permitted its members to hold diametrically opposed views on these matters?

I was yet more disturbed by the existence within Anglicanism of a "liberal" wing that calls in doubt the Godhead of Christ, His Virgin Birth, His miracles and His bodily Resurrection. St. Thomas's words rang in my ears: "My Lord *and my God!*" (John 20:28). I heard St. Paul saying to me: "If Christ is not risen, then our preaching is in vain and your faith is also in vain" (1 Cor. 15:14). For my own salvation I needed to belong to a Church which held fast with unwavering faithfulness to the primary Christian teachings concerning the Trinity and the Person of Christ. Where could I find such a Church? Not, alas! in Anglicanism. It did not have that continuity and fullness of living Tradition for which I was searching.

What, then, of Rome? In the 1950s, before the second Vatican Council, the obvious course – for any Catholic-minded member of the Church of England who was unhappy about Anglican "comprehensiveness" – was to become a Roman Catholic. Here is a Christian communion which, no less than the Orthodox Church, claims an unbroken continuity with the Apostles and the Martyrs, with the early Councils and the Fathers. What is more, here is a Church of Western culture. Why, then, look to Orthodoxy? Could not my search for living Tradition find its fulfillment much nearer at hand?

Yet, whenever I felt tempted to move Romewards, I hesitated. What held me back was not primarily the *Filioque*, although after reading Lossky I could see that this was important. The basic problem, however, was the papal claim to universal jurisdiction and infallibility. From my study of the early centuries of Christianity, it became clear to me that Eastern Fathers such as St. Basil the Great and St. John Chrysostom – and indeed Western Fathers such as St. Cyprian and St. Augustine –

understood the nature of the Church on earth in a manner radically different from the viewpoint of the first Vatican Council. The developed doctrine of Roman primacy, as I saw it, was simply not true to history. Papal centralization, especially from the eleventh century onwards, had gravely impaired the continuity of Tradition within the Roman communion. Only in the Orthodox Church could I secure what I was seeking: the life-giving and undiminished presence of the past.

My conviction that only within Orthodoxy could I find in its fullness an unbroken continuity with the Church of the Apostles and the Fathers was reinforced by two other aspects of Orthodoxy that I began increasingly to notice. The first was the prevalence of persecution and martyrdom within recent Orthodox experience – first under the Turks and then, in our own century, under Communism. Here was something that linked the Orthodox Church of modern times directly to the pre-Constantinian Church of the first three centuries. "My strength is made perfect in weakness," said Christ to St. Paul (2 Cor. 12:9); and I saw His words fulfilled again and again in Orthodox history since the fall of Byzantium.

Alongside those who underwent an outward and visible martyrdom of blood, there have also been countless others in Orthodoxy who have followed the humiliated Christ through a life of inner martyrdom: kenotic saints who displayed a gentle, generous and compassionate love, such as Xenia of St. Petersburg, Seraphim of Sarov, John of Kronstadt, and Nektarios of Aegina. I found the same kenotic compassion in the writings of Dostoevsky and Tolstoy. Two saints who especially appealed to me – for I had been a pacifist since the age of seventeen – were the Passion-Bearers Boris and Gleb, brother Princes from eleventh-century Kiev. In their refusal to shed blood even in self-defense, in their repudiation of violence and their innocent suffering, I saw exemplified the central message of Christ's Cross.

Another aspect of Orthodoxy which I came to value, alongside martyrdom, was the mystical tradition of the Christian East. Tradition, I realized, signifies not just the handing-down of doctrinal definitions but equally the transmission of spirituality. There cannot be any separation, and still less any opposition, between the two; as Vladimir Lossky rightly states, "there is... no Christian mysticism without theology; but, above all, there is no theology without mysticism," for mysticism is to be seen "as the perfecting and crown of all theology: as *theology par excellence*."[28]

Whereas it had been the liturgical services with their rich symbolism and their music that originally drew me to Orthodoxy, I now saw how this "iconic" form of worship is counterbalanced in the Christian East by the "non-iconic" or apophatic practice of hesychastic prayer, with its "laying-aside" of images and thoughts. In *The Way of a Pilgrim* and the writings of "A Monk of the Eastern Church" – Archimandrite Lev Gillet, the Orthodox chaplain of the Fellowship of St. Alban and St. Sergius – I learnt how *hesychia*, stillness or silence of the heart, is attained through the constant repetition of the Jesus Prayer. St. Isaac the Syrian showed me that all words find their fulfillment in stillness, just as servants fall silent when the master arrives in their midst:

> *Let every mouth and every tongue become silent.*
> *Let the heart which is the treasury of our thoughts,*
> *and the intellect which is the ruler of our senses,*
> *and the mind, that swift-winged and daring bird,*
> *with all their resources and powers and persua-*
> *sive intercessions – let all these now be still: for*
> *the Master of the house has come.*[29]

The Church as Communion

These three things – Tradition, martyrdom and stillness – were already sufficient to convince me of the truth and relevance of Orthodoxy. But the compelling need for me not only to contemplate Orthodoxy from the outside, but also to enter within, was brought home to me by words that I heard spoken in August 1956 at the summer conference of the Fellowship of St. Alban and St. Sergius. Father Lev Gillet was asked to define the term "Orthodoxy." He replied: "An Orthodox is one who accepts the Apostolic Tradition and who *lives in communion with the bishops* who are the appointed teachers of this Tradition."

The second half of this statement – the part which I have italicized – was of particular significance for me. I thought to myself: Yes, indeed, as an Anglican I am at liberty to hold the Apostolic Tradition of Orthodoxy as my own private opinion. But can I honestly say that this Apostolic Tradition is taught unanimously by the Anglican bishops with whom I

---

28 *The Mystical Theology of the Eastern Church* (London 1957), p. 9.

29 Isaac of Nineveh, *Homily* 23 (22): tr. A.J. Wensinck (Amsterdam 1923), p. 112; tr. Dana Miller (Holy Transfiguration Monastery, Boston 1984), p. 116.

am in communion? Orthodoxy, so I recognized in a sudden flash of insight, is not merely a matter of personal belief; it also presupposes outward and visible communion in the sacraments with the bishops who are the divinely commissioned witnesses of the truth. The question could not be avoided: If Orthodoxy means communion, was it possible for me to be truly Orthodox so long as I still remained an Anglican?

Those simple words spoken by Father Lev created no great stir in the Conference at large, but for me they served as a critical turning-point. The idea which they planted in my mind – that Orthodox faith is inseparable from Eucharistic communion – was confirmed by two things which I read around this time. First, I came across the correspondence between Alexis Khomiakov and the Anglican (as he was then) William Palmer, Fellow of Magdalen College, Oxford. Palmer had sent Khomiakov a copy of his work A *Harmony of Anglican Doctrine with the Doctrine of the Catholic and Apostolic Church of the East*. Here Palmer took, phrase by phrase, the *Longer Russian Catechism* written by St. Philaret of Moscow, and for every statement in the *Catechism* he cited passages from Anglican sources in which the same doctrine was affirmed. In his reply (28 November 1846), Khomiakov pointed out that he could equally well have produced an alternative volume, quoting other Anglican writers – no less authoritative than those invoked by Palmer – who directly contradicted the teaching of Philaret's *Catechism*. In Khomiakov's words:

> *Many Bishops and divines of your communion are and have been quite orthodox. But what of that? Their opinion is only "an individual opinion," it is not "the Faith of the Community." The Calvinist Ussher is an Anglican no less than the bishops (whom you quote) who hold quite Orthodox language. We may and do sympathize with the individuals; we cannot and dare not sympathize with a Church... which gives Communion to those "who declare" the Bread and Wine of the High Sacrifice to be mere bread and wine, as well as to those who declare it to be the Body and Blood of Christ. This for an example – and I could find hundreds more – but I go further. Suppose an impossibility – suppose all the Anglicans to be*

> *quite Orthodox; suppose their Creed and Faith quite concordant with ours; the mode and process by which that creed is or has been attained is a Protestant one; a simple logical act of the understanding.... Were you to find all the truth, you would have found nothing; for we alone can give you that without which all would be vain – the assurance of truth.*[30]

Khomiakov's words, severe yet just, reinforced what Father Lev had said. By this time I had come to believe all that the Orthodox Church believed; yet the "mode and process" by which I had reached these beliefs was indeed a "Protestant one." My faith was "only *an individual opinion*," and not "*the Faith of the Community*"; for I could not say that all my fellow Anglicans believed the same as I did, or that mine was the faith taught by all the Anglican bishops with whom I was in communion. Only by becoming a full member of the Orthodox Church – by entering into full and visible communion with the Orthodox bishops who were the appointed teachers of the Orthodox faith – could I obtain "the assurance of truth."

A few months later I read in typescript an article on the ecclesiology of St. Ignatius of Antioch by the Greek-American theologian Father John Romanides.[31] Here, for the first time in a fully developed form I encountered the perspective of "Eucharistic ecclesiology" which has since been popularized by the writings of Father Nicolas Afanassieff[32] and Metropolitan John (Zizioulas) of Pergamum.[33] On a first reading Father John's interpretation of the letters of St. Ignatius at once convinced me, and when I consulted the actual letters themselves my convictions were fully confirmed.

---

30 Birkbeck, *Russia and the English Church*, pp. 70-71 (quotes in the original).

31 This did not appear in print until several years later: see *The Greek Orthodox Theological Review* 7:1-2 (1961-2), pp. 53-77.

32 See N. Afanassieff, "The Church which Presides in Love," in John Meyendorff and others, *The Primacy of Peter* (London 1962), pp. 57-110 (new edition [St. Vladimir's Seminary Press, Crestwood 1992], pp. 91-143). Cf. Aidan Nichols, *Theology in the Russian Diaspora: Church, Fathers, Eucharist in Nikolai Afanas'ev (1893-1966)* (Cambridge 1989).

33 See John D. Zizioulas, *Being as Communion: Studies in Personhood and the Church* (London/New York 1985). Cf. Paul McPartlan, *The Eucharist Makes the Church: Henri de Lubac and John Zizioulas in Dialogue* (Edinburgh 1993).

The primary icon of the Church for St. Ignatius, so I found, was precisely this: a table; on the table, a plate with bread and wine; around the table, the bishops, the presbyters and the deacons, along with all the Holy People of God, united together in the celebration of the Eucharist. As St. Ignatius insisted, "Take care to participate in one Eucharist: for there is one flesh of our Lord Jesus Christ, and one cup for union in His blood, and one altar, just as there is one bishop."[34] The repetition of the word "one" is deliberate and striking: "one Eucharist... one flesh... one cup... one altar... one bishop." Such is St. Ignatius' understanding of the church and its unity: the Church is *local*, an assembly of all the faithful in the same place (*epi to avto*); the Church is *Eucharistic*, a gathering around the same altar, to share in a single loaf and a single cup; and the Church is *hierarchical* – it is not simply *any* kind of Eucharistic meeting, but it is that Eucharistic meeting which is convened under the presidency of the one local bishop.

Church unity, as the Bishop of Antioch envisages it, is not merely a theoretical ideal but a practical reality, established and made visible through the participation of each local community in the Holy Mysteries. Despite the central role exercised by the bishop, unity is not something imposed from outside by power of jurisdiction, but it is created from within through the act of receiving communion. The Church is above all else a Eucharistic organism, which becomes itself when celebrating the sacrament of the Lord's Supper "until He comes again" (1 Cor. 11:26). In this way St. Ignatius, as interpreted by Father John Romanides, supplied me with an all-essential missing link. Khomiakov had spoken about the organic unity of the Church, but he had not associated this with the Eucharist. Once I perceived the integral connection between ecclesial unity and sacramental communion, everything fell into place.

Yet where did this leave me, still (as I was) an outsider, unable to receive the Orthodox sacraments? At Easter 1957 for the first time I attended the Orthodox service at Paschal Midnight. I had intended to receive communion later in the morning at an Anglican church – in that year the dates of Orthodox and Western Easter coincided – but, emerging from the Orthodox celebration, I knew that this was an impossibility. I had already kept Christ's Resurrection with the Orthodox Church, in a manner that was for me complete and unrepeatable. Had I afterwards

---

34   *To the Philadelphians* 4.

received Holy Communion elsewhere, that would have been – for me personally – something unrealistic and untruthful.

Never thereafter did I make my communion at an Anglican altar. After remaining without the sacrament for some months, I was talking in September 1957 with Madeleine, the wife of Vladimir Lossky. She pointed out to me the peril of my situation, living as I was in no man's land. "You must not continue as you are," she insisted. "The Eucharist is our mystical food: without it, we starve."

Her words were confirmed a few days later by a strange incident that I have never been able fully to explain to myself. I went to the chapel in Versailles where the head of the Western European diocese of the Russian Church in Exile, Archbishop John (Maximovitch) – now glorified as a saint – was officiating at the Divine Liturgy. It was his custom to celebrate daily, and as it was a weekday there were very few present: only one or two monks, as I recall, and an old woman. I arrived near the end of the service, shortly before the moment when he emerged to give communion. No one came forward to receive the sacrament, but he remained standing with the chalice in his hand; and with his head on one side in his characteristic way, he stared fixedly and even fiercely in my direction (he had never seen me before). Only when I shook my head did he return to the sanctuary with the chalice.

After the conclusion of the Liturgy there was a service of intercession (*paraklesis, molieben*) in honour of the Saint whose day it was; and at the close the Archbishop anointed those present with oil from the lamp before the Saint's icon. I stayed where I was, not knowing if as a non-Orthodox it was appropriate for me to receive anointing. But this time he would accept no refusal. He beckoned firmly, and so I came forward and was anointed. Then I left the chapel, too shy to stay behind and speak with him (but we did meet and talk on future occasions).

St. John's action at the moment of communion puzzled me. I knew that, according to the practice of the Russian Church in Exile, anyone intending to receive communion is required first to go to confession. Surely, then, the Archbishop would have been warned if there were going to be any communicants. In any case, a prospective communicant – at least in a Russian church – would not have arrived so late during the service. The Archbishop was gifted with the power to read the secrets of the human heart; had he perhaps some intimation that I was on the threshold of Orthodoxy, and was this his way of telling me not to delay any longer?

Whatever the truth of the matter, my experience at Versailles strengthened my feeling that the moment had come for action. If Orthodoxy is the one true Church, and if the Church is a communion in the sacraments, then I needed above all else to become an Orthodox communicant.

Look not at things that are seen....

There remained, however, one powerful dissuasive. If Orthodoxy is really the one true Church of Christ on earth, how could it be (I asked myself) that the Orthodox Church in the West is so ethnic and nationalist in its outlook, so little interested in any form of missionary witness, so fragmented into parallel and often conflicting "jurisdictions"?

In principle, of course, Orthodoxy is indeed altogether clear about its claim to be the true Church. As I read in the message of the Orthodox delegates at the Assembly of the World Council of Churches in Evanston (1954):

> *In conclusion we are bound to declare our profound conviction that the Holy Orthodox Church alone has preserved full and intact "the Faith once delivered to the saints." It is not because of our human merit, but because it pleases God to preserve "His treasure in earthen vessels, that the excellency of the power may be of God" (2 Cor. 4:7).*[35]

Yet there seemed to be a yawning gap between Orthodox principles and Orthodox practice. If the Orthodox really believed themselves to be the one true Church, why did they place such obstacles in the path of prospective converts? In what sense was Orthodoxy truly "one," when, for example, in North America there were at least nineteen different Orthodox "jurisdictions," with no less than thirteen bishops in the single city of New York?[36] Some of my Anglican friends argued that the

---

35   In Constantin G. Patelos, *The Orthodox Church in the Ecumenical Movement. Documents and Statements 1902-1975* (Geneva 1978), p. 96. I imagine that Father Georges Florovsky was closely involved in drafting this fine statement. What a pity that Orthodox delegates at recent meetings of the WCC have not spoken with so clear a voice!

Orthodox Church was no more unified than the Anglican communion, and in some respects less so; if I moved, it would be out of the frying pan into the fire!

At this point I was helped by some words of Vladimir Lossky:

> *How many recognized in "the man of sorrows" the eternal Son of God? One must recognize the fullness there where the outward sense perceives only limitations and want.... We must, in the words of St. Paul, receive "not the spirit of the world, but the Spirit which is of God; that we may know the things that are freely given to us of God" (1 Cor. 2:12), that we may be enabled to recognize victory beneath the outward appearance of failure, to discern the power of God fulfilling itself in weakness, the true Church within the historic reality.*[37]

Looking at the empirical situation of twentieth-century Orthodoxy in the Western world, I was indeed confronted by apparent "failure" and weakness"; and the Orthodox themselves did not deny this. But, looking more profoundly, I could also see "the true Church within the historical reality." The ethnic narrowness and intolerance of Orthodoxy, however deep-rooted, are not part of the essence of the Church, but they are a distortion and betrayal of its true nature (of course there are also positive aspects to Orthodox Christian nationalism). As for the jurisdictional pluralism of the Orthodox Church in the West, this has specific historical causes; and the more visionary among Orthodox leaders have always seen it as at best a provisional arrangement that is no more than temporary and transitional. Moreover, there is an evident difference between the divisions prevailing within Anglicanism and those found within Orthodoxy. The Anglicans are united (for the most part) in outward organization, but deeply divided in their beliefs and in their forms of public worship. The Orthodox, on the other hand, are divided only in outward organization, but firmly united in beliefs and worship.

---

36   I give the figures for the year 1960, as found in the brochure *Parishes and Clergy of the Orthodox, and Other Eastern Churches in North and South America together with the Parishes and Clergy of the Polish National Catholic Church 1960-61*, edited by Bishop Lauriston L. Scaife and issued by the Joint Commission on Cooperation with the Eastern Churches of the General Convention of the Protestant Episcopal Church. I have not included the non-Chalcedonians in my calculations.

37   *The Mystical Theology of the Eastern Church*, pp. 245-6.

At this juncture I received a powerfully-worded letter from an English Orthodox priest with whom I was in correspondence, Archimandrite Lazarus (Moore), at that time resident in India. With reference to the Orthodox Church, he wrote:

> *Here I must warn you that the outward form of the church is desperately wretched, in a word cruci-fied, with little cooperation or coordination be-tween the various national bodies, little deep use and appreciation of our spiritual riches, little missionary and apostolic spirit, little grasp of the situation or of the needs of our times, little gener-osity or heroism or real sanctity. My advice is: Look not at the things that are seen....*[38]

I tried to follow Father Lazarus's guidance. Looking beyond the outward and visible failings of Orthodoxy, I made an act of faith in "the things that are not seen" (2 Cor. 4:18) – in its fundamental oneness, and in the underlying wholeness of its doctrinal, liturgical and spiritual Tradition.

In order to enter the Orthodox house, I had to knock upon a particular door. Which "jurisdiction" should I choose? I felt strongly drawn to the Russian Orthodox Church in Exile – the Russian Orthodox Church Outside Russia (ROCOR), as it is today commonly styled. What I admired in particular was its fidelity to the liturgical, ascetic and monastic heritage of Orthodoxy. While still sixteen I had come across Helen Waddell's book *The Desert Fathers*, and from that moment I was fascinated by the monastic history of the Christian East. I found that most of the monasteries in the Orthodox emigration belonged to the Russian Church in Exile. In Western Europe I visited two women's monasteries under its care, the Convent of the Annunciation in London, and the Convent of the Mother of God of Lesna outside Paris, and in both I was given a warm welcome. I also admired the way in which the Russian Church in Exile held in honour the New Martyrs and Confessors who had suffered for the faith under the Soviet yoke. On the other hand, I was disturbed by the canonical isolation of the Exile Synod. In the 1950s this was not so great as it has since become, for at that time there was still

---

38   Letter of 11 April 1957.

regular concelebration between Russian Exile clergy and the bishops and priests of the Ecumenical Patriarchate. But I saw that the Russian Church in Exile was becoming increasingly cut off from worldwide Orthodoxy, and that troubled me.

Had there existed in Britain a Russian diocese under the Ecumenical Patriarchate, as there was in France, then I would probably have joined it. As matters stood, the only Russian alternative to the Church in Exile was the Moscow Patriarchate. This had some distinguished members in Western Europe, such as Vladimir Lossky in Paris, Father Basil Krivocheine in Oxford, and Father Anthony Bloom (now Metropolitan of Sourozh) in London. But I felt it impossible to belong to an Orthodox Church headed by bishops under Communist control who regularly praised Lenin and Stalin, and who were prevented from acknowledging the New Martyrs slain by the Bolsheviks. I did not wish in any way to pass judgment on the ordinary Russian faithful dwelling inside the Soviet Union; they were under bitter persecution and I was not, and I do not suppose that in their situation I would have shown anything of the heroic endurance which they displayed. But, living as I did outside the Communist world, I could not make my own the statements issued by leading hierarchs of the Moscow Patriarchate in the name of the Church. As one of the Russian Exile priests in London, Archpriest George Cheremeteff, said to me: "In a free country we must be free."

Despite my love of Russian spirituality, it became evident to me that my best course was to join the Greek diocese in Britain under the Patriarchate of Constantinople. As a Classicist, I had a good working knowledge of New Testament and Byzantine Greek, whereas I had not studied Church Slavonic. If I became a member of the Ecumenical Patriarchate I would not have to take sides between the rival Russian groups, and I could maintain my personal friendships with members of both the Moscow Patriarchate and the Church in Exile. More importantly, Constantinople was the Mother Church from which Russia had received the Christian faith, and I felt it right in my quest for Orthodoxy to return to the source. Also I began to appreciate that, when eventually the Orthodox in Western Europe achieved organizational unity, this could only happen under the pastoral protection of the Ecumenical Throne.

So back I went to Bishop James of Apamaea, and much to my surprise I found him on this occasion willing to receive me almost at once. It is true that he warned me, "Please understand that we would *never*, under any circumstances, ordain you to the priesthood; we need only Greeks."[39] That did not worry me, for I was content to leave my future in the hands of God. I was only too delighted that the door had at last opened, and I entered without wishing to lay down any conditions. I saw my reception into Orthodoxy not as a "right," not as something that I was entitled to "demand," but simply as a free and unmerited gift of God's grace. It gave me quiet happiness when Bishop James appointed Father George Cheremeteff as my spiritual father, and so I was able to remain close to the Russian Church in Exile.

Thus I came to the end of my journey; or, more exactly, to a new and decisive stage on a journey which had begun in my earliest infancy and which, by the divine mercy, will continue into all eternity. Shortly after Pascha in 1958, on Friday in Bright Week – The Feast of the Life-Giving Source – I was chrismated by Bishop James at the Greek Cathedral of St. Sophia in Bayswater, London. At last I had come home.

Father Lazarus had warned me that I would find in the Orthodox Church "little generosity or heroism or real sanctity." In retrospect, after nearly four decades as an Orthodox, I can say that he was much too pessimistic. Doubtless I have been more fortunate than I deserve, but within Orthodoxy I have in fact found warm friendship and compassionate love almost everywhere that I have gone, and I have certainly enjoyed the privilege of meeting living saints. Those who predicted that, in becoming Orthodox, I would be cutting myself off from my own people and my national culture have been proved wrong. In embracing Orthodoxy, so I am convinced, I have become not less English but more genuinely so; I have rediscovered the ancient roots of my Englishness, for the Christian history of my nation extends back to a period long before the schism between East and West. I remember a conversation that I had with two Greeks soon after my reception. "How hard you must find it," remarked the first, "to have left the Church of your fathers." But the second said to me, "You did not leave the Church of your fathers: you returned to it." He spoke rightly.

Needless to say, my life as an Orthodox has not always been "heaven on earth." Repeatedly I have suffered deep discouragement; but did not Jesus Christ Himself foretell that discipleship means cross-bearing? Yet,

---

39   In fact I was ordained priest in 1966, eight years after my reception, by Metropolitan (later Archbishop) Athenagoras of Thyateira, who had arrived in Britain in 1963/64.

forty-four years later, I can affirm with all my heart that the vision of Orthodoxy which I saw at my first Vigil Service in 1952 was sure and true. I have not been disappointed.

I would make only one qualification: what I could not have appreciated back in 1952, but what today I see much more clearly, is the deeply enigmatic character of Orthodoxy, its many antitheses and polarities. The paradox of Orthodox life in the twentieth century is summed up by Father Lev Gillet, himself a Westerner who made the journey to Orthodoxy, in words which come closer to the heart of the matter than any others that I can recall:

> *O strange Orthodox Church, so poor and so weak... maintained as if by a miracle through so many vicissitudes and struggles; Church of contrasts, so traditional and yet at the same time so free, so archaic and yet so alive, so ritualistic and yet so personally mystical; Church where the Evangelical pearl of great price is preciously safeguarded – yet often beneath a layer of dust.... Church which has so frequently proved incapable of action – yet which knows, as does no other, how to sing the joy of Pascha!*[40]

---

40   Father Lev Gillet, in Vincent Bourne, *La Queste de Verité d'Irénée Winnaert* (Geneva 1966), p. 335.

Biographies of Contributors

BARLOW, WILLIAM is a former professional soldier, having served in the Irish Guards. After leaving the Army he took part in pioneering work in the field of juvenile delinquency before undertaking training for the Anglican priesthood. A post-graduate scholarship enabled him to study the Orthodox Church in Greece. He became Orthodox on return to England. He has worked extensively on educational projects for foreign students under the auspices of the YMCA. He has also undertaken many speaking engagements as well as broadcasting for the BBC. His account of how he became Orthodox, *Intent Only on Life*, is published by Harper Collins. He is married to a Bostonian and lives in London.

BERNSTEIN, FR. A. JAMES was born May 6, 1946 in Lansing, Michigan of Orthodox Jewish parents. He grew up in New York City and in 1960 won the US Junior Chess Championship (under 16 years of age division). At sixteen he became an Evangelical Protestant Christian after reading the New Testament. While in Jerusalem, Israel in 1967 the Six Day War broke out. Following the war he was among the first to move into the Old City, living where his father had been born. On returning to America, he received his BA in 1970 from Queens College in New York City. Following graduation, he moved to the San Francisco Bay Area with Moise Rosen, where he helped found "Jews for Jesus" and became active in the "Jesus Movement" of the 1970s. In 1975 he was ordained a minister in the Evangelical Orthodox Church. In 1981 he converted to canonical Orthodoxy (OCA). Returning to NYC with his wife, Bonnie (who is a midwife) and four children, he attended St. Vladimir's Seminary from 1985 to 1989 and received the M. Div. degree. On July 10, 1988 he was ordained priest in the Antiochian Archdiocese. Since 1990, Father James has served and led the building of a new church-temple near Seattle, Washington called Saint Paul Orthodox Church. He has written a booklet, published by Concilliar Press: *Orthodoxy: Jewish and Christian*. A second work, also to be published by Concilliar Press, will address itself to the question: "What came first, the Church or the New Testament?"

FOREST, JAMES HENDRICKSON. Born in Utah in November 1941, Jim Forest grew up in New Jersey and California. In 1958 he joined the Navy and worked at the US Weather Bureau in Washington, DC. In November 1960 he was received into the Catholic Church. After being discharged as a conscientious objector in the summer of 1961, he joined the Catholic Worker community in New York City and later became managing editor of its newspaper. A founder of Pax (later Pax Christi USA). In 1963 he was managing editor of *Liberation* magazine and the following year a journalist with *The Staten Island Advance*. From 1965 to 1967, he was secretary of the Catholic Peace Fellowship and a reporter for Religious News Service. In 1967 he became Special Projects Secretary for the Fellowship of Reconciliation, responsible for Vietnam-related programs. In 1968, as part of a group that burned draft records in Milwaukee, Wisconsin, he was imprisoned for 13 months. He was a member of the Emmaus Community in East Harlem, New York City, in 1971-72, and taught at New York Theological Seminary and the College of New Rochelle. In 1973 he headed the Thomas Merton Center at the Cathedral of St. John the Divine, New York City. From 1974 to 1976, he was editor of *Fellowship*, magazine of the Fellowship of Reconciliation. In 1977 he was appointed General Secretary of the International Fellowship of Reconciliation in Alkmaar, Holland. He remained with IFOR until 1988. While on sabbatical in 1985, he taught at the Ecumenical Institute, Tantur, near Jerusalem. He was received into the Orthodox Church at St. Nicholas of Myra Russian Orthodox Church, Amsterdam on Palm Sunday, 1988. Since 1988 he has been a freelance writer. He also edits Peace Media Service and, with his wife Nancy, is co-secretary of the Orthodox Peace Fellowship. He is the author of various books, including *Living With Wisdom* (a biography of Thomas Merton), *Love is the Measure* (a biography of Dorothy Day), *Religion in the New Russia*, *Pilgrim to the Russian Church*, and *Making Friends of Enemies*.

FOREST-FLIER, NANCY. Nancy Forest-Flier grew up in northern New Jersey where she and her family were active in the Dutch Reformed Church. She attended Hope College in Holland, Michigan, a Reformed Church institution, and in 1971 graduated *cum laude* with a bachelor's degree in English literature. After graduation she worked at the national office of the Fellowship of Reconciliation in Nyack, New York. In order to pursue an interest in typesetting and type editing she left the FOR in 1980 to take a job in a New York typesetting shop. In 1982 she left the United States to marry Jim Forest, who was living and working in the Netherlands. Nancy, Jim and their five children have been residents in the Netherlands since that time. Nancy works as a free-lance writer, editor and translator. In 1988 she and Jim were received into the Russian Orthodox Church. They are members of the Church of St. Nicholas of Myra in Amsterdam.

LONG, MARGARET VISCOUNTESS (Nee Frazer) was born in Singapore, Malaya, where her father was a Scottish Rubber Planter. Her mother died when she was a year old and her father was taken prisoner by the Japanese in World War II. She was brought up and educated in Scotland until leaving for London in her late teens in order to study music. Descendant of an old Scottish family. One ancestor was George Bogle, an eighteenth century Glasgow merchant who was the first white man ever to stay in Tibet. Her great uncle was Sir James Frazer O.M the Cambridge scholar and author of *The Golden Bough*. She married into the English Aristocracy in 1957 and her husband became Lord in Waiting to Her Majesty the Queen. Three children, one of whom was killed tragically in a car accident in 1984, three days before her nineteenth birthday. From about 1978 onwards Lady Margaret has had a series of mystical experiences which culminated in a conversion to Orthodoxy in 1986 when both she and her eldest daughter, Sarah were taken into the Russian Orthodox Church in London by Metropolitan Anthony of Sourozh and Father John Lee. Now a freelance writer, she lives with her family in an old Manor House in the village of Castle Combe in Wiltshire.

MATHESON, FR. CHARLES DANIEL. A native of Nova Scotia, Canada, Fr. Daniel received his B. A. in 1940 from Dalhousie University, Halifax, Nova Scotia. He received his M. Div. degree from Pine Hill Divinity Hall (now Atlantic School of Theology) also in Halifax. In 1967 The United Theological College of Montreal, Canada conferred on him the degree of Doctor of Divinity (*honoris causa*). He was ordained into the ministry of The United Church of Canada in 1942, and was the pastor of congregations in Nova Scotia, Prince Edward Island, Manitoba,

Toronto and Ottawa — all in Canada. In 1985 he was received into the Evangelical Orthodox Church. In 1987 he was ordained to the priesthood of the Orthodox Church by His Grace, Bishop Antoun of The Antiochian Orthodox Christian Archdiocese. He and his wife Vera are the parents of a daughter and two sons. He serves as a semi-retired assistant priest in St. Elijah Orthodox Church in Ottawa, Canada.

NEWMAN, PROFESSOR BARBARA. A native of Chicago, Barbara Newman was born to Jewish parents and baptized into the Episcopal Church at the age of 19. She was educated at Oberlin College, the University of Chicago, and Yale, where she received her Ph.D. in Medieval Studies in 1981. While researching her dissertation in London, she received instruction at the Russian Orthodox Cathedral in Ennismore Gardens and was chrismated by Metropolitan Anthony of Sourozh. A specialist in medieval Western spirituality, she has edited and translated the poetry of Hildegard of Bingen (*Symphonia*) and is the author of *Sister of Wisdom: St. Hildegard's Theology of the Feminine* and *From Virile Woman to WomanChrist: Essays on Medieval Religion and Literature*. Professor Newman chairs the English Department at Northwestern University and is a member of Holy Trinity Cathedral in Chicago. She lives in Evanston with her husband, Richard Kieckhefer, and two wickedly beautiful cats.

SISTER NONNA was born Verna Harrison in New Haven, Connecticut to an old American family whose lineage has been traced back to the original Jamestown settlement in Virginia in 1619. She grew up in suburban Los Angeles and studied at Yale University, where she received her B.A. in philosophy and political science in 1974. She was awarded a Ph.D. in patristics at the Graduate Theological Union in Berkeley in 1986. She has published numerous scholarly articles on the Fathers of the Church and on Orthodox theology, and in 1992 a book on *Grace and Human Freedom According to St. Gregory of Nyssa*. She has taught in the Late Vocations Program of the Diocese of the West, (OCA), for several years. In Spring Semester 1993, she taught patristics at St. Vladimir's Seminary, and is currently teaching the same subject at St., Joseph of Arimathea Anglican Theological College in Berkeley. Many parishes and institutions have asked her to lead retreats and to give public lectures in the recent past. On April 1st she was tonsured a *rassophone* nun and given the name of the mother of Saint Gregory the Theologian.

KALLISTOS WARE, BISHOP OF DIOKLEIA. Since his first major work, *The Orthodox Church* in 1963, Bishop Kallistos, the pre-eminent Orthodox theologian in the English-speaking world, has explained, promoted, and made accessible significant texts such as *The Festal Menaion* and *The Lenten Triodio*n (with Mother Mary), and *The Philokalia* with G.E.H. Palmer and Philip Sherrard. He has lectured widely throughout the world and published many monographs. Based in Oxford, England, he is a member of the Fellowship of St. Alban and St. Sergius and on the Advisory Board of the Orthodox Peace Fellowship.